GROW UP YOUR IDEA & MINDSET

BHUPENDRA SINGH

First published by Notion Press Media Pvt. Ltd. 2025

ISBN 979-889984163-7
Self Help / Business / Entrepreneurship

Printed and bound in India by
Notion Press Media Pvt. Ltd.

To My Parents,
For Everything

Preface

If you're holding this book, chances are you're already someone who believes in the power of **growth**. You're not content to simply exist; you want to expand, to evolve, to make a real impact. That's fantastic, because this book was written for you.

For years, I've had the privilege of sharing insights on personal development with millions of readers around the world. My previous works explored the foundations of success, the art of building resilience, and the quiet power of daily habits. But as I engaged with so many of you, I noticed a recurring theme, a question that resonated deeper than the others: "How do I take my ideas—those nascent sparks of potential—and truly bring them to life, while simultaneously cultivating a mindset that supports audacious growth?"

That question became the genesis of *Grow Up Your Idea & Mindset*. This isn't just another book on motivation; it's a practical guide to **transforming your inner world to shape your outer reality**. We'll delve into the fascinating interplay between the ideas that flicker within you and the mindset that either fuels their ascent or clips their wings.

We'll explore why some brilliant ideas never see the light of day, while others—seemingly less revolutionary—blossle into groundbreaking innovations.

The secret, as you'll discover, lies not just in the quality of the idea itself, but in the **fertile ground of your mind**. We'll unearth the hidden beliefs that might be holding you back, and equip you with the tools to cultivate a mindset of unwavering optimism, relentless curiosity, and unshakeable belief in your own potential.

This journey won't always be easy. Growth, by its very nature, can be uncomfortable. It demands introspection, challenges assumptions, and often asks us to step beyond what feels safe and familiar. But I promise you this: the rewards are immeasurable. You'll learn to **nurture your ideas from conception to creation**, to **pivot with grace in the face of setbacks**, and to **embrace every challenge as an opportunity for profound learning**.

My hope is that *Grow Up Your Idea & Mindset* serves as your trusted companion on this exciting adventure. It's packed with actionable strategies, relatable anecdotes, and exercises designed to spark your creativity and rewire your thinking. Whether you're an entrepreneur with a world-changing concept, a creative yearning to express yourself fully, or simply someone eager to unlock their untapped potential, this book will provide the roadmap.

It's time to stop just dreaming about your ideas and start *growing* them. It's time to stop letting limiting beliefs define you and start *cultivating* a mindset that empowers you to achieve the extraordinary. Let's grow, together.

-Bhupendra Singh, Author

Table of Contents

Introduction

The Seed of Potential

Every great achievement, every groundbreaking innovation, every personal transformation begins with a single, often fragile, thing: an idea. It might be a whisper in the quiet of your mind, a sudden flash of insight, or a persistent nagging feeling that there's a better way. But an idea, on its own, is just a seed. For it to blossom into something tangible, something impactful, it needs fertile ground, consistent nourishment, and the right environment to flourish.

And that fertile ground, my friend, is your **mindset**.

In a world that constantly bombards us with information, demands, and distractions, it's easy to feel overwhelmed. We might have brilliant ideas, but they get lost in the noise, or worse, they're stifled by self-doubt, fear of failure, or the paralyzing belief that we're not "good enough" to bring them to fruition. This book is here to tell you that those limiting beliefs are not your destiny. They are merely weeds in the garden of your potential, and with the right tools and understanding, you can clear them away, making space for extraordinary growth.

For years, my work has focused on the principles of personal development, helping individuals unlock their potential and live more fulfilling lives. Through countless conversations, workshops, and interactions with readers like you, one truth has become abundantly clear: **the quality of your ideas is inextricably linked to the quality of your mindset.** You can have the most revolutionary concept, but if your mind is cluttered with negativity, fixed beliefs, or a fear of stepping outside your comfort zone, that idea will likely remain dormant. Conversely, even a simple idea, when nurtured by a growth-oriented, resilient, and curious mind, can achieve remarkable things.

This book, *Grow Up Your Idea & Mindset*, is designed to be your comprehensive guide on this transformative journey. We're not just going to talk about abstract concepts; we're going to dive deep into actionable strategies that you can implement immediately.

You'll learn to:

- **Understand Why Your Ideas Matter:** Discover the profound impact your unique ideas can have, not just on your own life, but on the world around you. We'll explore how to identify the ideas that truly resonate with your purpose and passion.

- **Embrace the Power of a Growth Mindset:** This isn't just a buzzword; it's a fundamental shift in how you perceive challenges, failures, and your own capabilities. You'll learn to cultivate resilience, optimism, and an insatiable hunger for learning, turning every setback into a stepping stone.

- **Uncover What You'll Discover in This Book:** We'll systematically break down the process of nurturing both your inner world and your outward creations. From identifying and challenging limiting beliefs to practical techniques for idea generation, prototyping, and sustained action, each chapter builds upon the last, guiding you towards a life where your ideas not only survive but thrive.

This is more than just a book; it's an invitation. An invitation to look inward, to cultivate the richest soil for your dreams, and to unleash the incredible potential that lies within you. It's time to stop waiting for inspiration to strike and start actively growing your ideas and, most importantly, growing yourself.

Are you ready to plant the seeds of your future?

Let's begin.

Part 1

Cultivating the Fertile Ground (Mindset)

Chapter 1
Unearthing Your Core Beliefs

In the introduction, we established that your mindset is the fertile ground where your ideas either flourish or wither. Now, it's time to dig a little deeper into that soil. Before we can plant new seeds of possibility, we must first understand the existing landscape, particularly the roots of our beliefs. Many of these roots are hidden, buried deep beneath the surface of our conscious awareness, yet they exert an immense influence on our thoughts, actions, and ultimately, our ability to grow our ideas.

Identifying Limiting Beliefs

Think for a moment about a time you had a great idea, felt a surge of excitement, and then, almost immediately, a wave of doubt washed over you. Perhaps a voice in your head whispered, "That's too ambitious," or "You're not smart enough," or "What will people think?" These are the echoes of **limiting beliefs**.

Limiting beliefs are deeply ingrained convictions that we hold about ourselves, others, or the world, which restrict our potential and prevent us from taking action. They are often formed in childhood, through experiences, observations, or messages we receive from authority figures, peers, or even media. While they might have served a protective function at some point (e.g., "Don't try new things, it's safer"), they can become significant barriers to growth in adulthood. Consider how a seemingly innocent comment from a teacher about your artistic ability could, over decades, solidify into the belief "I'm not creative." Or how a single failed attempt at a new venture might lead to the pervasive thought, "I'll fail if I try." These beliefs are not necessarily based on objective truth, but rather on interpretations and conclusions drawn from past experiences, often reinforced by societal norms or comparisons to others. They manifest subtly, often as procrastination, self-sabotage, or a general reluctance to pursue opportunities that push you beyond your perceived limits.

Common limiting beliefs include:

- *"I'm not creative."* (Perhaps you tried painting once and didn't like the result, internalizing it as a lack of innate talent.)
- *"I'm not good enough."* (This can stem from constant comparison or a feeling of inadequacy in various areas of life.)
- *"I don't have enough time/money/resources."* (Often a convenient excuse that masks a deeper fear of commitment or effort.)
- *"It's too late for me."* (A belief that age or past opportunities define your future potential.)
- *"I'll fail if I try."* (A fear of failure so strong that it prevents any attempt at all.)

- *"What if others judge me?"* (The fear of external validation or criticism stifling authentic expression.)
- *"I'm not a natural leader."* (Despite having great ideas, this belief might prevent you from stepping up.)
- *"Success is only for a select few."* (A belief that your circumstances or background preclude you from achieving greatness.)

The first step to transforming these beliefs is to identify them. Pay close attention to your inner dialogue, especially when you're contemplating a new idea or stepping outside your comfort zone. What are the immediate thoughts that arise? What excuses do you find yourself making? What fears are bubbling up? Write them down. Don't judge them; simply acknowledge their presence. This act of bringing them into the light is the first step towards disarming their power. Think of yourself as a detective, observing your thoughts without attachment, simply noting their patterns and recurring themes. The more you practice this self-awareness, the clearer the picture of your underlying beliefs will become.

The Neuroscience of Belief

Our brains are incredible pattern-matching machines. When we repeatedly think a certain thought or experience a particular emotion, our neural pathways strengthen, making it easier for us to default to those same thoughts and feelings in the future. This is why limiting beliefs can feel so stubbornly persistent – they have well-worn neural highways in our minds. Imagine a path through a dense forest: the more you walk it, the clearer and easier it becomes to traverse. Similarly, a belief like "I'm not good at public speaking" becomes a deeply grooved neural pathway.

Every time you avoid a speaking opportunity, or feel anxious about one, you're inadvertently strengthening that belief, making it the default response. Your brain, in its efficiency, simply takes the path of least resistance.

Conversely, when you believe "I can learn and improve," you're building different, more empowering pathways. This is where the concept of **neuroplasticity** comes into play. Neuroplasticity is the brain's remarkable ability to reorganize itself by forming new neural connections throughout life. It's not a fixed organ; it's dynamic and adaptable. Every time you learn something new, practice a skill, or even change your perspective, you are literally rewiring your brain. Old, unhelpful pathways can weaken through a process called "synaptic pruning" (where unused connections are trimmed away), while new, beneficial ones are strengthened. This means that your beliefs are not fixed, immutable facts; they are patterns of thought that can be changed through conscious effort and consistent practice. Your brain is a muscle, and just like any muscle, it can be trained to become stronger and more flexible in the ways that serve you.

Rewiring Your Inner Dialogue

Now that you've identified some of your limiting beliefs and understand the brain's capacity for change, the next crucial step is to actively **rewire your inner dialogue**. This isn't about simply ignoring negative thoughts; it's about consciously replacing them with empowering ones, systematically building those new, stronger neural pathways. This process requires patience and persistence, but the results are profoundly liberating.

Here are practical strategies for rewiring your inner dialogue:

1. **Challenge the Evidence:** When a limiting belief surfaces, don't just accept it. Become a skeptical investigator. Ask yourself: "Is this absolutely, 100% true in every single situation? What concrete evidence do I have to support this belief? Is there any evidence, no matter how small, that contradicts it?" For example, if the thought is "I'm not good at networking," recall any instance, however brief, where you had a positive interaction with someone new. Even a simple "Hello" that went well is evidence against the absolute statement. Look for exceptions, not just confirmations. Often, you'll find that the "evidence" is based on isolated past failures, outdated assumptions, or even someone else's opinion, not your current reality or future potential.

2. **Reframe Your Thoughts:** This is about consciously shifting your perspective. Instead of "I can't do this," try "How *can* I do this?" or "What steps can I take to learn how to do this?" Instead of "This is too hard," try "This is a challenge I can learn from and grow through." Shift from a fixed mindset ("I am incapable of X") to a growth mindset ("I can *become* capable of X through effort and learning"). For instance, if you think, "I messed up that presentation," reframe it to, "That presentation was a learning experience. What can I improve next time?" This subtle shift moves you from self-criticism to constructive analysis.

3. **Use Affirmations (Wisely):** Affirmations are positive statements repeated regularly to reinforce new beliefs. However, they must feel authentic and resonate with you. Don't say "I am a millionaire" if you don't genuinely believe it, as your subconscious will resist. Start with something more believable and process-oriented, like "I am capable of attracting abundance through my efforts" or "I am consistently learning how to manage my finances effectively." Focus on the *process* of growth and the actions you can take. Repeat them daily, perhaps while looking in a mirror, or write them down. The key is consistency and believing in the *possibility* of the statement, even if the full reality isn't there yet.

4. **Practice Visualization:** Your brain often can't distinguish between a vividly imagined experience and a real one. Use this to your advantage. Close your eyes and vividly imagine yourself successfully achieving what your limiting belief says you can't. See yourself speaking confidently, launching your idea with ease, or gracefully overcoming a challenge. Engage all your senses: What do you see, hear, feel? What emotions are you experiencing? The more detailed and emotionally resonant your visualization, the more effectively you build those new, empowering neural pathways. Do this regularly, especially before situations that trigger your limiting beliefs.

5. **Mindful Awareness:** This is about catching yourself in the act of negative self-talk. When you hear that familiar limiting voice, simply acknowledge it without judgment. Don't fight it or get angry at yourself for having the thought. Instead, observe it, perhaps even label it ("Ah, there's that 'not good enough' thought again"), and then consciously choose a different, more empowering thought. Think of your thoughts as clouds passing in the sky; you can observe them without needing to cling to them. This takes consistent practice, but with time, you'll become more adept at interrupting the old patterns and redirecting your mental energy.

6. **"As If" Principle:** Start acting "as if" you already possess the belief you want to cultivate. This is about embodying the desired state. If you want to believe you're a confident speaker, prepare thoroughly, dress professionally, make eye contact, and stand tall. If you want to believe you're a successful entrepreneur, start taking the actions a successful entrepreneur would take – networking, planning, iterating. Your actions can powerfully influence your beliefs, creating a positive feedback loop where doing leads to believing, which in turn fuels more doing.

Unearthing and transforming your core beliefs is a foundational step in growing both your ideas and your mindset. It requires patience, persistence, and a willingness to be honest with yourself. This isn't a one-time fix but an ongoing practice. There will be days when old beliefs resurface, but with the strategies outlined here, you are now equipped to challenge them, reframe them, and consciously choose the thoughts that serve your highest potential. By consistently choosing to challenge what holds you back and cultivate empowering new thoughts, you are laying the groundwork for unprecedented personal and creative growth. The next chapter will build on this by exploring how to embrace optimism and resilience, turning every challenge into a stepping stone.

Chapter 2

The Art of Optimism and Resilience

In Chapter 1, we explored the foundational work of unearthing and rewiring limiting beliefs. You've begun to understand that your thoughts are not fixed entities but malleable pathways in your brain. Now, we build on that foundation by cultivating two indispensable qualities for growth: **optimism** and **resilience**. These aren't just pleasant traits; they are powerful tools that enable you to navigate the inevitable challenges of bringing your ideas to life and sustaining your personal evolution.

Embracing Challenges as Opportunities

It's a common misconception that optimists are simply people who ignore problems or live in a state of perpetual naiveté. True optimism, especially in the context of a growth mindset, is far more robust. It's not about denying reality, but about **perceiving challenges not as roadblocks, but as opportunities for learning, innovation, and deeper understanding.** This distinction is critical: naive optimism might lead one to believe problems won't arise, while growth-oriented optimism accepts that problems *will* arise, but views them as solvable puzzles and valuable teachers. It's the difference between hoping for no storms and learning to sail skillfully through them.

Consider the journey of any successful entrepreneur, artist, or innovator. Their path is rarely a straight line. It's filled with detours, dead ends, and moments that test their resolve. Think of the countless prototypes that fail before a successful product emerges, or the rejections an author faces before finding a publisher, or the years an athlete trains for a single moment. What differentiates those who succeed from those who give up? Often, it's their ability to reframe setbacks. When an idea faces rejection, a project hits a snag, or a personal goal feels out of reach, the fixed mindset sees an insurmountable barrier, a sign to quit. The growth mindset, fueled by optimism, asks:

- "What can I learn from this experience? What hidden data or insight has this failure revealed?"
- "How can this challenge make my idea stronger? Perhaps this obstacle forces a necessary pivot or refinement."
- "What new skills can I develop by overcoming this? Is there a knowledge gap I need to fill, or a new approach I need to master?"
- "Is there a different approach I haven't considered yet? Could this be an invitation to innovate outside the box?"

This reframing is a conscious act, a deliberate mental shift. It involves stepping back from the immediate emotional reaction of frustration or disappointment and deliberately seeking the lesson or the hidden advantage. Perhaps a failed prototype reveals a critical flaw in your design or market assumption that, if discovered later, would have been far more costly in terms of time, resources, and reputation. Perhaps a rejection from one client or investor frees you up to pursue a more aligned and ultimately more rewarding opportunity that you wouldn't have otherwise considered.

Embracing challenges as opportunities means actively searching for the silver lining, the pivot point, or the unexpected benefit that can emerge from difficulty. It's about cultivating a proactive, rather than reactive, stance towards adversity, understanding that every challenge carries the seeds of an equal or greater advantage. This perspective doesn't just reduce stress; it actively enhances your problem-solving capacity, allowing your brain to shift from a threat response to a creative solution-seeking mode.

Building Mental Fortitude

Optimism is the lens through which you view challenges; **resilience** is the muscle that allows you to push through them. Mental fortitude is the capacity to withstand or recover quickly from difficulties, to bend without breaking. It's not about being fearless; it's about acknowledging fear and acting despite it. It's not about avoiding pain or discomfort; it's about enduring it, learning from it, and emerging stronger and wiser on the other side. This inner strength is forged in the fires of adversity, not in their absence.

How do you build this mental fortitude? It's a process, not an event, and it involves several key practices that you can integrate into your daily life:

1. **Develop a Strong "Why":** When your ideas face adversity, your "why" – your core purpose, your passion, the impact you want to make, the problem you want to solve – becomes your unshakeable anchor. Imagine you're building a groundbreaking app designed to connect isolated elderly individuals. When funding falls through or a technical bug seems insurmountable, simply remembering the faces of those who will benefit from your app can reignite your drive. Remind yourself constantly of the deeper reason behind your efforts. This intrinsic motivation provides the unwavering fuel to keep going when external circumstances are discouraging, when the path ahead seems unclear, or when doubts creep in. If your "why" is strong enough, the "how" will eventually reveal itself, often through creative and unexpected means.

2. **Practice Self-Awareness and Emotional Regulation:** The first step to managing your emotional response to challenges is to recognize it. Pay attention to how frustration, anger, or defeat manifest in your body

and mind. Instead of suppressing these emotions, which can lead to burnout or destructive coping mechanisms, acknowledge them. Say to yourself, "I'm feeling frustrated right now, and that's okay." Then, consciously choose how you respond. This might involve taking a short break to clear your head, practicing mindfulness through deep breathing exercises, or engaging in an activity that recharges you, like a short walk or listening to music. Emotional regulation isn't about eliminating negative emotions, but about preventing them from spiraling into destructive thought patterns or impulsive actions. It's about creating a healthy space between stimulus and response.

3. **Focus on What You Can Control:** Many challenges involve elements outside your control – market fluctuations, competitor actions, global events, or the opinions of others. Dwelling on these uncontrollable factors can be paralyzing, draining your energy and fostering a sense of helplessness. Instead, consciously shift your focus to the aspects you *can* influence. Can you adjust your strategy? Can you learn a new skill to better address the problem? Can you seek advice from someone who has faced similar challenges? Can you refine your message or product? By directing your energy towards actionable steps and internal levers, you regain a sense of agency, reduce feelings of helplessness, and

channel your efforts productively. This is the essence of proactive problem-solving.

4. **Embrace Discomfort:** Growth happens outside your comfort zone. Resilience is built not by avoiding discomfort, but by intentionally stepping into situations that challenge you, even if they feel awkward, intimidating, or slightly painful. Each time you push past a perceived limit – whether it's learning a new software, speaking up in a meeting, or tackling a complex project – you expand your capacity for future challenges. Start small; perhaps it's initiating a conversation with a stranger, trying a new exercise, or spending an hour on a task you've been procrastinating. Celebrate each step, no matter how minor, and gradually increase the intensity of your "discomfort training." This consistent, incremental exposure builds your tolerance for uncertainty and difficulty.

5. **Learn from Role Models:** Identify individuals who embody resilience and optimism, both in your personal life and in the broader public sphere. Study their stories. How did they overcome adversity? What strategies did they employ? What was their mindset when facing seemingly insurmountable odds? This could be a historical figure like Nelson Mandela, a contemporary leader, an artist who persevered through rejection, or even a friend or

family member who has navigated significant challenges with grace. While your journey is unique, there's immense wisdom to be gained from observing and internalizing the approaches of those who have navigated similar paths successfully. Read biographies, watch documentaries, or simply engage in conversations with resilient people.

Bouncing Back Stronger

The true test of resilience isn't whether you fall, but how quickly and effectively you get back up. Bouncing back stronger means more than just returning to your previous state; it means integrating the lessons learned from the setback and using them to propel you forward with greater wisdom, enhanced capabilities, and renewed determination. It's about transforming adversity into advantage.

This process of "bouncing back stronger" involves several critical steps:

- **Post-Mortem Analysis, Not Self-Blame:** When something doesn't go as planned, resist the urge to immediately blame yourself or others. Instead, conduct an honest, objective assessment – a "post-mortem." What went wrong? What specific decisions or actions contributed to the outcome? What external factors played a role? What could have been done differently in the future? Crucially, do this without resorting to self-criticism, shame, or dwelling on perceived failures. The goal is learning and improvement, not punishment or self-flagellation. Consider creating a "lessons learned" document for significant setbacks, detailing what happened, what was learned, and what actions will be taken moving forward. This transforms a negative event into a valuable data point for future success.

- **Adjusting Your Sails, Not Abandoning Ship:** A setback often signals that your current approach isn't working as effectively as it could. This is an opportunity to adjust your strategy, refine your idea, or seek new resources, rather than an imperative to give up entirely. It doesn't necessarily mean your idea is inherently flawed or that you are incapable; it means the path needs recalibration. Perhaps your initial marketing strategy was off, your product needed a different feature, or your timeline was unrealistic. Be flexible and adaptable. This might involve revising your business model, changing the scope of a project, learning a new skill, or even seeking a different target audience. The wind hasn't stopped blowing; you just need to adjust your sails to catch it better.

- **Seeking Support:** You don't have to go it alone. One of the hallmarks of truly resilient individuals is their willingness to reach out for help. Connect with mentors who have navigated similar challenges, trusted friends who offer a listening ear, or a supportive community that understands your journey. Sharing your struggles can provide new perspectives, emotional support, and practical advice you might not have considered. Sometimes, simply vocalizing your challenges to someone who listens without judgment can lighten the emotional load and help you see solutions more clearly. Remember, asking for help is a sign of strength, not weakness.

- **Celebrating Small Victories:** In the midst of a challenging period or after a significant setback, it's easy to lose sight of any progress. Make a conscious, deliberate effort to acknowledge and celebrate small wins, even tiny steps forward. Did you make one phone call you were dreading? Did you complete a small task that moved your idea forward? Did you learn a new concept? These mini-celebrations are vital. They release dopamine in your brain, reinforcing positive neural pathways and providing crucial motivation to keep going, especially when the overall goal seems distant. They remind you that you are capable of making progress, even when the overall journey feels arduous.

- **Practicing Self-Care:** Resilience is not about endlessly pushing yourself beyond your limits until you break. On the contrary, it requires periods of rest, rejuvenation, and intentional self-nurturing. Ensure you are prioritizing fundamental self-care practices: adequate sleep, nutritious food, regular physical exercise, and engaging in activities that bring you genuine joy and relaxation. This might also include setting healthy boundaries, taking digital detox breaks, pursuing hobbies unrelated to your main goal, or spending time in nature. A depleted mind and body are significantly less capable of handling stress, problem-solving creatively, and bouncing back effectively from adversity. Self-care is not a luxury or an indulgence; it's a fundamental component of sustained resilience and long-term growth.

Optimism and resilience are not innate traits reserved for a lucky few. They are dynamic skills that can be developed, strengthened, and refined through conscious practice and consistent effort.

By embracing challenges as opportunities, systematically building your mental fortitude, and learning to bounce back stronger from every setback, you create an inner environment where your ideas are not just protected from adversity, but actively thrive and evolve because of it. This robust mindset will serve as your unwavering companion as you continue to cultivate an insatiable curiosity and embrace lifelong learning, further enriching the fertile ground of your mind, which we will explore in the next chapter.

Chapter 3
Fueling Curiosity and Lifelong Learning

Having cultivated optimism and resilience, you've built a robust inner framework capable of weathering challenges and seeing opportunities in adversity. Now, it's time to infuse that framework with an insatiable hunger for knowledge and a commitment to continuous evolution. This chapter focuses on **fueling curiosity and embracing lifelong learning** – two qualities that are not merely beneficial, but absolutely essential for anyone looking to grow their ideas and expand their mindset in an ever-changing world.

Curiosity is the engine of discovery, the spark that ignites innovation. It's the innate human drive to explore, question, and understand. Without it, new ideas remain dormant, and existing ones stagnate. Lifelong learning, on the other hand, is the fuel that keeps that engine running, ensuring you remain adaptable, relevant, and endlessly capable of generating, refining, and successfully executing powerful ideas. It's the deliberate and voluntary pursuit of knowledge for personal or professional reasons, a continuous journey of expanding your intellectual horizons.

The Beginner's Mind

In Zen Buddhism, there's a profound concept called *Shoshin*, or "beginner's mind." It refers to having an attitude of openness, eagerness, and lack of preconceptions when studying a subject, even when studying at an advanced level, just as a true beginner would. This isn't about being ignorant; it's about consciously suspending what you think you already know to make space for new insights. This principle is profoundly relevant to growing your ideas and mindset, as it directly counters the intellectual inertia that can set in with expertise.

As we gain expertise in a particular area, whether it's coding, marketing, writing, or even parenting, there's a natural, almost unconscious tendency to become rigid in our thinking. We develop mental models, established processes, and a comfortable sense of "knowing." We rely on heuristics and past successes. While expertise is undeniably valuable and necessary for efficiency, it can sometimes inadvertently close us off to new possibilities, alternative solutions, or even the fundamental flaws in our existing approaches. An expert might dismiss a novel approach because "that's not how it's done," while a beginner, unburdened by such preconceptions, might stumble upon a revolutionary method. Think of how many industries were disrupted by outsiders who didn't know the "rules" and therefore weren't limited by them.

The beginner's mind, however, encourages us to:

- **Approach every situation with fresh eyes:** Imagine you're encountering a problem, a concept, or even your own long-held idea for the very first time. What questions would you ask if you had no prior knowledge? What assumptions would you instinctively challenge? This perspective can reveal novel solutions, overlooked connections, or hidden opportunities that an "expert" might miss due to ingrained patterns of thought and a tendency to categorize new information into existing frameworks. It allows you to see the forest *and* the trees.

- **Be willing to be wrong:** A true beginner isn't afraid to ask "dumb" questions or make mistakes, because they inherently expect to learn and grow. They understand that errors are integral to the learning process, not a reflection of their intelligence or capability. This intellectual humility is a superpower. It allows you to experiment freely without the crushing fear of failure, gather honest feedback without defensiveness, and iterate rapidly on your ideas. When you're not invested in being "right," you're free to be effective.

- **Embrace uncertainty and ambiguity:** The world of new ideas, innovation, and personal growth is inherently uncertain and often ambiguous. There are no guarantees, and clear paths are rarely laid out. The beginner's mind thrives in this ambiguity, seeing it not as a threat to be avoided, but as a vast, unexplored landscape ripe for exploration and discovery. It cultivates a comfort with the unknown, transforming anxiety into anticipation.

- **Listen more than you speak:** When you adopt a beginner's mindset, you naturally become a better, more active listener. You absorb information and diverse perspectives without immediately filtering them through your existing biases, judgments, or the need to formulate a response. This deep listening allows for genuine understanding and the assimilation of truly novel insights, rather than simply confirming what you already believe.

Cultivating a beginner's mind means intentionally stepping outside your comfort zone of established knowledge and intellectual habits. It might involve learning a completely new, seemingly unrelated skill (e.g., a programmer taking up pottery, a writer studying astrophysics), exploring a different industry's best practices, or simply asking "why" repeatedly about something you thought you already understood. This deliberate act of intellectual humility keeps your mind agile, flexible, and endlessly receptive to new insights, preventing stagnation and fostering a continuous state of growth. It's about recognizing that even the most seasoned expert has more to learn, and that true mastery lies not in knowing everything, but in the perpetual, joyful pursuit of knowledge and understanding.

Seeking Knowledge and Inspiration

Curiosity is the internal drive, the innate desire to know. But seeking knowledge and inspiration is the active, deliberate pursuit of satisfying that drive. In today's interconnected, information-rich world, information is abundant, but discerning valuable, relevant knowledge and finding genuine, actionable inspiration requires intentional effort and strategic engagement. This isn't just about formal education or academic pursuits; it's about building a holistic lifestyle of continuous learning and intellectual nourishment.

Here are diverse, powerful avenues for seeking knowledge and inspiration:

1. **Read Widely and Deeply:** Beyond books directly related to your primary field or interests, make a conscious effort to explore diverse genres, non-fiction on seemingly unrelated topics, biographies of influential figures, and even fiction that expands your empathy, creativity, and understanding of the human condition. Reading exposes you to different ways of thinking, problem-solving methodologies, and storytelling

structures. Make reading a non-negotiable part of your daily or weekly routine, even if it's just 15-30 minutes. Consider reading outside your comfort zone – if you're a scientist, pick up a philosophy book; if you're an artist, delve into economics or ancient history. This "cross-pollination" of ideas from disparate fields often sparks the most innovative and unexpected breakthroughs, as you begin to see connections where others see none.

2. **Engage in Diverse Conversations:** Your network is a powerful source of knowledge. Actively seek out people from different backgrounds, industries, cultures, and perspectives than your own. Attend conferences, join online communities, participate in workshops, or simply initiate genuine conversations with people you wouldn't normally interact with. Every person you meet holds a unique library of experiences, insights, and perspectives. Practice asking open-ended questions, listen actively without formulating your next response, and be genuinely curious about their worldviews, challenges, and successes. These interactions can profoundly challenge your assumptions, expose you to new paradigms, and provide unexpected angles or solutions for your ideas.

3. **Consume Varied Media Mindfully:** Beyond traditional reading, leverage the vast array of

modern media. Explore thought-provoking podcasts, insightful documentaries, structured online courses (MOOCs), expert interviews, and even well-curated newsletters. The key here is **mindful consumption** – don't just passively absorb information. Take notes, pause to reflect on what you're learning, and actively consider how it connects to your existing knowledge, current ideas, or professional challenges. Use these resources strategically to fill specific knowledge gaps, explore emerging trends, and stay abreast of developments that could impact your field or spark entirely new directions for your work. Curate your information diet to be rich and varied.

4. **Travel and Experience New Cultures:** Stepping outside your familiar environment, whether it's your city, country, or even your daily routine, is a profoundly powerful way to gain new perspectives. Travel exposes you to different ways of life, problem-solving approaches, social structures, and expressions of creativity. Even if extensive international travel isn't feasible, explore local communities, visit museums, attend cultural festivals, or try new cuisines that are outside your norm. Immersion in different contexts broadens your understanding of human needs, desires, and challenges, which can be invaluable for developing relevant, impactful, and universally appealing ideas. It pushes you to adapt and observe, fostering a deeper sense of global awareness.

5. **Experiment and Play:** Learning isn't solely about absorbing information; it's about active engagement and hands-on exploration. Dedicate dedicated time to experimentation, even if it seems unproductive or without an immediate goal. Tinker with new tools, try a new hobby (e.g., coding if you're a writer, painting if you're an engineer), or simply allow yourself to "play" with ideas without the pressure of immediate results or perfection. This playful, low-stakes exploration often leads to unexpected discoveries, strengthens your intuitive understanding, and fosters a sense of creative freedom. Many groundbreaking inventions and artistic movements came from playful curiosity and accidental discoveries rather than rigid adherence to a predetermined plan. Think of the Post-it Note, discovered by accident, or penicillin.

6. **Seek Mentorship and Coaching:** Learning from those who have walked the path before you is an accelerated form of knowledge acquisition. A mentor can offer guidance, share hard-won lessons, and provide a roadmap for navigating challenges. A coach can help you unlock your own potential, identify blind spots, and hold you accountable for your learning and growth goals. These relationships provide personalized insights and accelerate your development in ways that self-study alone cannot.

Adapting to Change

The only constant in life is change. This adage has never been more relevant than in our current era, where technological advancements, global interconnectedness, and societal shifts occur at an unprecedented pace. In such a rapidly evolving world, the ability to adapt is not just an advantage; it is paramount for survival and growth. Curiosity and lifelong learning are the bedrock of adaptability. When you are continuously learning, you are not caught off guard by shifts in technology, market trends, or societal needs. Instead, you are prepared to pivot, innovate, and even lead the change, rather than being a victim of it.

Consider the implications of a fixed mindset in a dynamic environment: resistance to adopting new technologies, clinging stubbornly to outdated methods that once worked, or dismissing emerging trends as fads. This leads inevitably to stagnation, irrelevance, and ultimately, obsolescence. Think of companies like Blockbuster, which failed to adapt to streaming, or traditional media outlets that resisted the digital revolution. Their fixed mindsets led to their decline. A growth mindset, however, fueled by an active curiosity and a commitment to continuous learning, sees change as:

- **An opportunity for reinvention:** Each shift, disruption, or new development presents a chance to re-evaluate your existing ideas, refine your approach, or even discover entirely new avenues for impact and value creation. It's a call to innovate.

- **A call to acquire new skills:** Instead of fearing obsolescence or feeling threatened by new technologies, you embrace the challenge of learning what's next. This proactive approach keeps you valuable, versatile, and highly employable in any field. You become a lifelong student of your craft and the world around you.
- **A chance to lead:** Those who are quick to learn, synthesize new information, and adapt their strategies are often the ones who become the innovators, thought leaders, and pioneers in their fields. They don't just react to the future; they actively shape it, anticipating trends and positioning themselves at the forefront of change.

Adapting to change isn't just about reacting to what has already happened; it's about anticipating what's coming. It involves staying informed through your diverse learning habits, cultivating a network that provides diverse insights and early warnings, and being willing to let go of what no longer serves your growth, even if it was once successful. It means understanding that your ideas, like living organisms, must evolve to survive and thrive. A rigid idea in a fluid world is destined to break under pressure. The more you learn, the more connections you can make, and the better equipped you are to see opportunities where others see only threats.

By actively fueling your curiosity and committing to lifelong learning, you transform yourself into a perpetual student of life. This not only enriches your personal world, expands your perspective, and keeps your mind vibrant, but also equips you with the intellectual agility, creative capacity, and strategic foresight needed to grow your ideas into their fullest, most impactful potential, no matter how rapidly the landscape shifts. In the next chapter, we will delve into the often-overlooked yet critical practice of self-compassion, ensuring your growth journey is sustainable, kind, and truly holistic.

Chapter 4
The Power of Self-Compassion

You've embarked on a powerful journey, cultivating optimism, resilience, and an insatiable hunger for learning. These are formidable strengths, equipping you to face the external world with courage and an open mind. Yet, there's one more crucial element to fortify your mindset, an internal resource that often goes overlooked: **self-compassion**. This isn't about self-pity, making excuses for inaction, or letting yourself off the hook for genuine mistakes. Instead, it's about treating yourself with the same kindness, understanding, and encouragement you would instinctively offer a dear friend, a beloved family member, or even a child facing similar challenges and setbacks. In the demanding pursuit of growing ideas, navigating complex projects, and fostering continuous personal development, self-compassion is the quiet superpower that ensures your journey is not only sustainable but also deeply joyful, creatively effective, and ultimately, more successful. It acts as an emotional buffer, allowing you to learn from adversity without being crushed by it, and to persevere with a gentle yet firm resolve.

Silencing the Inner Critic

We all possess an inner critic. For some, it manifests as a subtle, nagging whisper of doubt, a faint background hum of inadequacy. For others, it's a booming, relentless voice of judgment and condemnation, a constant barrage of "shoulds" and "shouldn'ts." This inner critic often originates from a place that *believes* it's helping us improve – a misguided attempt to protect us from perceived threats or failures by pointing out every flaw. However, its methods are typically harsh, unconstructive, and ultimately counterproductive. It tells us we're not good enough, smart enough, or capable enough. It magnifies every minor misstep into a catastrophic failure and minimizes every hard-won success, often whispering, "That was just luck," or "Anyone could have done that." If left unchecked, this relentless internal assault can erode confidence, stifle nascent creativity, paralyze action, and effectively sabotage your most earnest efforts to grow your ideas and expand your potential. It can lead to perfectionism that prevents completion, procrastination born of fear, and a deep sense of unworthiness.

The inner critic thrives on a toxic cocktail of perfectionism, an exaggerated fear of failure, and the insidious habit of constant comparison with others. It often speaks in absolute, black-and-white terms, devoid of nuance: "You *always* mess this up," or "You'll *never* be as good as them," or "This idea is stupid." Silencing this critic doesn't mean eliminating it entirely – after all, it's a deeply ingrained part of your brain's protective and evaluative mechanisms, however misguided its current expression. Instead, the goal is to fundamentally change your relationship with it, to disarm its power and transform its influence.

Here's how to begin to silence, or at least reframe, your inner critic:

1. **Recognize the Voice:** The absolute first step is heightened self-awareness. When you hear a harsh, judgmental thought directed at yourself, pause. Don't immediately accept it as truth. Instead, notice it as a distinct thought. Pay attention to the specific language it uses – is it accusatory, dismissive, or shaming? Notice any physical sensations that accompany it, like tension in your shoulders or a knot in your stomach. Then, ask yourself a critical question: "Is this a thought I would ever say to someone I care about, someone I respect and want to see succeed?" The answer, almost invariably, will be no. This recognition creates a crucial psychological distance between "you" (your authentic self) and "the critic's voice" (a pattern of thought).

2. **Externalize the Critic:** To further detach from its grip, give your inner critic a name, or imagine it as a separate, distinct entity. This helps you realize it's

not *you* speaking your truth, but rather a specific, often unhelpful, part of your mind. You might call it "Perfectionist Pete," "The Doubter," "My Fear Monster," or "The Taskmaster." When that familiar negative thought arises, you can then say, "Oh, there's 'Perfectionist Pete' acting up again," or "My 'Fear Monster' is trying to scare me." This simple act of externalization, of personifying the voice, can significantly reduce its power and allow you to observe it rather than be consumed by it. It shifts you from being the victim of the criticism to the observer of it.

3. **Challenge Its Authority:** Just as you learned to challenge limiting beliefs in Chapter 1, apply the same rigorous questioning to the critic's pronouncements. Don't blindly accept its statements as facts. Ask: "Is that really, absolutely true? What concrete, verifiable evidence do I have to support this belief? Is there *any* evidence, no matter how small, that contradicts it?" For instance, if the critic says, "You *always* mess up presentations," recall even one presentation where you did well, or even just one slide that went smoothly. Often, the critic's statements are gross exaggerations, overgeneralizations, or outright falsehoods based on past insecurities rather than current reality. This process of seeking evidence helps dismantle the critic's false authority.

4. **Respond with Kindness and Reason:** Instead of fighting the critic, which often gives it more power, respond to it with a compassionate, rational, and firm voice – the voice of your wise, supportive self. If it says, "You're a failure because that project didn't work," you might respond, "I made a mistake on that project, and it didn't go as planned, but I'm learning valuable lessons from it, and that's a crucial part of the growth process. I am doing my best, and that is enough." Or, "This is tough, and I'm feeling challenged, but I am capable of figuring this out." This isn't about being Pollyannaish; it's about acknowledging the reality of the situation while simultaneously extending understanding and encouragement to yourself. This consistent practice of compassionate self-talk actively builds new, more positive neural pathways in your brain, gradually weakening the old, critical ones.

5. **Focus on Effort, Not Just Outcome:** The inner critic often fixates exclusively on results, especially negative ones, and demands perfection. To counteract this, consciously shift your focus to the effort you put in, the learning that occurred, and the process you engaged in, regardless of the immediate outcome. Remind yourself that growth is a journey, not a destination. If a creative project didn't turn out as envisioned, acknowledge the effort you invested in learning a new technique or pushing through a

difficult phase. This shift in focus is crucial for maintaining motivation and building long-term resilience, as it teaches your brain to value perseverance and learning over immediate, perfect results.

Learning from Mistakes, Not Dwelling on Them

Mistakes are not just inevitable; they are an essential, indeed invaluable, part of growth, learning, and innovation. Every successful innovation, every personal breakthrough, every mastery of a skill, is built on a foundation of countless attempts that didn't quite work out as planned. Think of Thomas Edison's thousands of experiments before the lightbulb, or J.K. Rowling's numerous rejections before *Harry Potter* became a phenomenon. Yet, our society often heavily stigmatizes mistakes, viewing them as signs of incompetence or failure, leading us to fear them and, when they happen, to dwell on them with crippling shame, regret, and self-recrimination. Self-compassion allows you to transform mistakes from sources of anguish and paralysis into powerful, actionable learning opportunities.

When you inevitably make a mistake:

- **Acknowledge the Pain:** It's a natural human response to feel disappointment, frustration, sadness, or even anger when something goes wrong, especially if you've invested significant effort or hope. Don't try to suppress or ignore these emotions.

Self-compassion means validating your own experience and emotional reality. Say to yourself, "This hurts, and that's a natural, understandable reaction to this setback. It's okay to feel this way." Allowing yourself to feel these emotions, without judgment, is the first step towards processing them and moving forward.

- **Practice Common Humanity:** One of the core tenets of self-compassion is the recognition of common humanity. Remind yourself that making mistakes is a universal human experience. Every single person, no matter how intelligent, successful, or seemingly perfect, makes errors. You are not alone in this. Your mistake doesn't make you uniquely flawed or incompetent. This perspective helps you feel less isolated in your struggle and less like a unique failure, fostering a sense of connection rather than shame. It shifts the internal narrative from "What's wrong with *me*?" to "This is a difficult human experience that many people face."

- **Investigate, Don't Incriminate:** Once you've acknowledged the emotional impact, shift into a curious, analytical mode. Instead of asking, "What's wrong with me? Why am I such a failure?" ask, "What happened here? What was the sequence of events? What was the process I followed? What specific factors contributed to this outcome? What could be done differently next time?" Approach the mistake with the objective curiosity of a scientist analyzing an experiment that yielded unexpected results, rather than a judge presiding over a criminal trial. Document your findings, identify root causes, and brainstorm alternative approaches. The goal is learning and improvement, not punishment or self-flagellation.

- **Focus on Repair and Moving Forward:** Once you've extracted the valuable lessons from the mistake, shift your energy decisively to what you can do to rectify the situation (if possible) and how you can apply the learning to future endeavors. Dwelling on the past without a constructive purpose is unproductive and emotionally draining. Self-compassion allows you to release the shame and regret associated with the past and channel your energy into purposeful action. This might involve apologizing, making amends, revising a plan, or simply committing to a new approach. The focus is always on forward momentum, armed with new wisdom.

Celebrating Small Wins

In our relentless pursuit of ambitious goals and grand ideas, it's remarkably easy to overlook, dismiss, or simply forget to acknowledge the myriad small victories along the way. Yet, celebrating these "micro-successes" is incredibly important for sustaining motivation, reinforcing positive habits, building robust self-belief, and counteracting the brain's natural negativity bias. It's a direct, powerful antidote to the inner critic, which often dismisses anything less than absolute perfection as insignificant. Each small win, when recognized, releases dopamine in the brain, a powerful neurotransmitter associated with pleasure, motivation, and reward.

This creates a positive feedback loop, encouraging you to repeat the actions that led to that feeling of accomplishment.

Celebrating small wins involves:

- **Conscious Recognition:** Make a deliberate, mindful effort to notice and acknowledge every step forward, no matter how minor it may seem. Did you complete a difficult task you've been procrastinating on? Did you learn a new concept that expands your understanding? Did you make tangible progress on a challenging project, even if it was just one small component? Did you simply show up and put in the effort on a day you felt unmotivated? These are all wins.

- **Internal Acknowledgment:** Give yourself a genuine mental pat on the back. Use positive self-talk: "Well done, I really pushed through that!" or "I'm proud of that effort and the progress I made." This internal validation is profoundly powerful. It builds your internal locus of control and reinforces your sense of capability, independent of external praise.

- **Small Rituals:** Create simple, personal rituals to mark these moments. The ritual doesn't have to be elaborate or time-consuming; its significance comes from the conscious act of acknowledgment and the consistency of its practice. This could be a quick stretch or a short walk around the block, listening to a favorite upbeat song, taking a five-minute break to enjoy a cup of tea, writing down the win in a "success journal," or sharing your progress with a supportive friend, mentor, or accountability partner. The ritual acts as a psychological bookmark, signaling to your brain that something positive has occurred.

- **Connecting to the Bigger Picture:** See how each small win contributes directly to your larger goals and the overall growth of your idea and mindset. Each completed task, each new piece of knowledge acquired, each challenge overcome, is a vital brick in the foundation of your growing idea and evolving self. Visualizing this cumulative progress helps maintain perspective and reinforces the value of consistent effort, even when the ultimate destination still seems distant. It transforms seemingly insignificant steps into meaningful milestones.

Celebrating small wins isn't about becoming complacent or resting on your laurels; it's about building momentum, reinforcing positive neural pathways, and creating a sustainable wellspring of motivation. It trains your brain to seek and appreciate progress, fostering a positive feedback loop that encourages you to keep going, even when the path ahead seems long or arduous.

Self-compassion, then, is not a weakness but a profound strength. It is the act of extending kindness, understanding, and acceptance to yourself, especially in moments of perceived inadequacy, failure, or suffering. It's the gentle yet firm hand that guides you through the inevitable bumps, detours, and outright crashes on the road of growth, allowing you to learn, adapt, and persevere without succumbing to harsh self-judgment or burnout. By actively working to silence your inner critic, learning constructively from every mistake, and celebrating every step of progress, you build an inner sanctuary of unwavering support that empowers you to truly grow your ideas and mindset with grace, resilience, and unwavering determination. You become your own most powerful ally. In the next part of the book, we will shift our focus from cultivating your inner world to the practical strategies for nurturing your ideas from conception to creation, building on the strong foundation of mindset you've now established.

Part 2

Nurturing Your Ideas (Idea Development)

Chapter 5

From Spark to Concept: Idea Generation

Having spent the first part of this book fortifying your inner world—cultivating optimism, building resilience, fueling curiosity, and embracing self-compassion—you are now primed for the exciting, often exhilarating, work of bringing your ideas to life. This marks the beginning of **Part 2: Nurturing Your Ideas (Idea Development)**. The journey from a fleeting thought, a mere glimmer of possibility, to a tangible, well-defined concept is a thrilling one, fraught with challenges but rich with potential. And it all begins with the foundational act of **idea generation**. This initial phase is where the raw material for innovation is unearthed, where vague notions start to take shape, and where the boundless expanse of possibility begins to narrow into focused potential.

Many people mistakenly believe that great ideas are born from a sudden, singular flash of genius, a "Eureka!" moment that strikes out of the blue, reserved only for a select few creative savants. While such moments of sudden insight do indeed occur, they are rarely isolated incidents. More often, they are the culmination of prolonged observation, deep curiosity, persistent questioning, and consistent effort in exploring a problem space.

True idea generation is less about passively waiting for divine inspiration or lightning to strike and more about actively creating the conditions for it to appear. It's a skill that can be honed, a muscle that can be strengthened through deliberate practice, and a process that can be systematized. By understanding the fertile grounds from which ideas spring and employing proven techniques, you can transform yourself into a prolific idea generator.

Where Do Great Ideas Come From?

If you've ever felt frustrated by a perceived lack of "good ideas," or found yourself staring at a blank page, you are certainly not alone. This feeling often stems from a misunderstanding of how ideas actually form. The truth is, truly great ideas rarely emerge in a vacuum, fully formed and perfect. Instead, they are typically the result of a dynamic process: connecting disparate dots, observing deeply felt unmet needs, diligently solving persistent problems, or creatively reimagining and improving upon existing solutions. They often arise at the unique intersection of your personal experiences, accumulated knowledge, diverse skills, and genuine passions. This intersection is your unique vantage point, offering perspectives others may not have.

Here are some common, yet incredibly potent, wellsprings of impactful ideas, along with deeper insights into how to tap into them:

1. **Solving Personal Pain Points:** The most authentic, resonant, and often most impactful ideas frequently come from challenges you or someone very close to you has personally faced. What genuinely frustrates you in your daily life, professionally or personally? What routine task feels unnecessarily complicated, inefficient, or annoying? What product or service do you constantly wish existed but doesn't, or doesn't exist in a way that truly serves your needs? For example, the founders of Airbnb, Brian Chesky and Joe Gebbia, weren't initially trying to revolutionize hospitality; they simply needed a way to pay their rent in San Francisco and saw an opportunity in renting out air mattresses during a design conference. This addressed a very personal, immediate pain point that, as it turned out, resonated globally with both travelers seeking affordable accommodation and hosts looking to monetize spare space. Your own frustrations, no matter how minor they seem, can be the clearest, most authentic signal to an unmet need that, once solved for yourself, can be scaled to help many others. Keep a "frustration journal" to capture these moments.

2. **Observing Unmet Needs in Others:** Moving beyond your personal experience, cultivate a keen sense of observation for the complaints, inefficiencies, and desires of people around you – your friends, family, colleagues, customers, or even strangers you

encounter. Listen actively to their gripes, watch how they navigate their daily lives, and pay attention to where they express dissatisfaction or longing. What do they struggle with repeatedly? What tasks do they find tedious, time-consuming, or difficult? What do they wish they had more of – time, convenience, joy, peace of mind? Conduct informal "ethnographic research" by simply watching and listening without judgment. A parent constantly complaining about the difficulty of finding healthy, appealing snacks for their kids might spark an idea for a new line of nutritious, child-friendly food products. A small business owner expressing exasperation with managing their social media presence might inspire a new, simplified consulting service or software solution.

The key is empathy: putting yourself in their shoes and feeling their pain points.

3. **Identifying Gaps in Existing Solutions:** Take a critical, yet constructive, look at current products, services, or processes that are widely used. Are they perfect? Almost certainly not. Where are the shortcomings, the inefficiencies, the areas ripe for improvement? What could be made faster, cheaper, more user-friendly, more aesthetically pleasing, more sustainable, more inclusive, or simply more effective? This is the essence of iterative innovation – building upon what already exists. Think of how

countless successful apps and services have emerged not by inventing something entirely new, but by simply making an existing service more convenient, accessible, or delightful. For example, ride-sharing apps like Uber and Lyft didn't invent transportation; they identified significant gaps and frustrations in the traditional taxi service model (difficulty hailing, inconsistent pricing, poor customer experience) and offered a technologically enhanced, more convenient alternative. This requires a discerning eye for detail and a willingness to question the status quo.

4. **Leveraging Your Unique Skills and Passions:** What are you naturally good at? What specific skills have you honed through education, work, or hobbies? What topics genuinely excite you, so much so that you lose track of time when engaging with them? What do you love to do, even if you're not paid for it? Your unique blend of talents, experiences, and interests is a powerful differentiator and a rich source of authentic ideas. An idea that aligns with your deep passion will provide an unparalleled wellspring of intrinsic motivation, sustaining you through the inevitable challenges and setbacks. A web developer who is also a passionate fitness enthusiast might create an innovative workout tracking app that combines their technical prowess with their understanding of fitness needs. A history enthusiast with strong research and storytelling

skills might develop a unique educational platform that makes complex historical narratives engaging and accessible. When your passion meets a market need, that's where true magic happens.

5. **Connecting Disparate Fields/Ideas (Combinatorial Creativity):** Many truly revolutionary ideas and inventions come from taking a concept, principle, or technology from one domain and applying it in a completely different, seemingly unrelated context. This is often called "combinatorial creativity" or "idea cross-pollination." Can a principle from biological systems (e.g., swarm intelligence) be applied to business strategy or logistics? Can a design aesthetic from architecture be used to inform the user interface of software development? The printing press, a transformative invention, wasn't created from scratch; Johannes Gutenberg combined existing technologies like wine presses (for pressure) and coin punches (for individual letters) to create something entirely new and revolutionary. This requires broad curiosity, a willingness to read widely, and a deliberate practice of seeing connections where others see only unrelated elements. Actively seek out knowledge in diverse fields and then consciously look for analogies or transferable principles.

6. **Anticipating Future Trends:** Stay rigorously informed about emerging technologies, significant

societal shifts, demographic changes, and evolving environmental concerns. What problems will inevitably arise in the future as these trends accelerate? What needs will become more pronounced or even entirely new? For instance, a keen awareness of climate change and resource scarcity might lead to innovative ideas for sustainable energy solutions, circular economy business models, or eco-friendly consumer products. Similarly, understanding the aging global population could spark ideas for elder care technology, accessible design, or new forms of community engagement. This is about being proactive and thinking ahead, positioning yourself to solve tomorrow's problems today, rather than reacting to them when they become urgent. It requires foresight and a willingness to speculate intelligently about the future.

Brainstorming Techniques

Once you understand where ideas originate, the next crucial step is to actively generate them in a structured yet uninhibited way. Brainstorming is a powerful tool for this, but it's often done poorly, with premature judgment stifling the creative flow. The absolute key to effective brainstorming is to rigorously **separate idea generation from idea evaluation**. In the initial, generative phase, **quantity over quality** is paramount. No idea is too silly, too outlandish, too obvious, or too impractical to be recorded. The goal is to uncork the flow of thought, create a safe space for wild ideas, and capture absolutely everything that comes to mind. The more ideas you generate, the higher the probability of uncovering a truly brilliant one.

Here are proven techniques to supercharge your brainstorming sessions, whether you're working alone or with a group:

1. **Free Association/Brain Dump:** This is one of the simplest yet most effective methods. Set a timer for a short, focused period (e.g., 5-10 minutes). With a pen and paper, or a digital document, write down every single idea, thought, keyword, question, or even fragment that comes to mind related to your problem or area of interest. Do not stop writing, do not edit, do not judge, and do not self-censor. If you get stuck, write "I'm stuck" until another thought emerges. The goal is to exhaust your immediate, conscious thoughts and then push past them. This often uncovers hidden connections, unexpected directions, and truly novel insights once the obvious or conventional ideas are out of the way. The sheer act of continuous writing can unlock deeper creative reservoirs.

2. **Mind Mapping:** This visual technique encourages non-linear thinking and helps you see connections.

Start with your core problem, question, or topic in the very center of a large piece of paper (or a digital mind-mapping tool). From this central idea, branch out with related concepts, keywords, questions, potential solutions, or sub-topics. Use different colors, images, symbols, and varying line weights to make visual connections and emphasize relationships between ideas. Mind mapping leverages your brain's natural ability to think in associations, often revealing new avenues, categories, or relationships you hadn't consciously considered, creating a rich visual landscape of possibilities.

3. **SCAMPER Method:** This is a powerful, systematic checklist for transforming and innovating upon existing ideas, products, or services. It provides specific prompts to help you look at a concept from multiple angles and generate new variations. Apply these prompts to an existing concept, even a simple one, to force new perspectives:

    o **S**ubstitute: What can be substituted? (e.g., ingredients, materials, processes, people, places, time, other products/services). *Example: Substitute sugar in a recipe with a natural sweetener; substitute in-person meetings with virtual ones.*

    o **C**ombine: What can be combined? (e.g., features, ideas, services, purposes, talents, materials). *Example: Combine a phone with a camera (smartphone); combine a coffee shop with a bookstore.*

- **A**dapt: What can be adapted? (e.g., from another context, a different industry, a historical solution, a natural phenomenon). *Example: Adapt a queuing system from a theme park to a hospital waiting room; adapt bird flight mechanics for drone design.*

- **M**odify (Magnify/Minify): What can be modified? Made bigger, smaller, different shape, color, stronger, weaker, faster, slower? *Example: Magnify a small component to be a standalone product; minify a large device for portability.*

- **P**ut to another use: How can it be used differently? For another purpose? For another target audience? *Example: Baking soda used for cleaning; old tires used for playground equipment.*

- **E**liminate: What can be removed, simplified, or reduced? (e.g., features, steps, costs, waste, effort). *Example: Eliminate physical buttons on a device; simplify a complex legal document.*

- **R**everse/Rearrange: What if you did the opposite? Changed the order? Reversed the process? Turned it inside out? *Example:*

> *Reverse the traditional sales process (customer finds you); rearrange furniture in a room for a new flow.*

4. **Worst Idea Brainstorming:** This counterintuitive technique can be incredibly effective at breaking mental blocks and fostering a more playful, less self-conscious approach to idea generation. Instead of trying to come up with "good" ideas, intentionally brainstorm the *worst* possible ideas for a given problem or challenge. This often leads to laughter, reduces the pressure of perfection, and can sometimes, surprisingly, lead to truly good ideas by simply reversing the "worst" elements. For example, if you're trying to improve customer service, a "worst idea" might be "make customers wait on hold for an hour while listening to terrible music." Reversing that might lead to "offer immediate callback options with personalized music choices." It's a powerful way to loosen up rigid thinking.

5. **Role Storming:** Imagine you are someone else – a child, a famous celebrity, a direct competitor, a historical figure, a person from a completely different industry, or even an alien. How would *they* approach this problem or idea? What unique perspective would they bring? This technique helps you step outside your own ingrained biases, assumptions, and typical modes of thinking,

unlocking entirely different solution pathways. For instance, how would a minimalist designer approach a complex software interface? How would a kindergarten teacher design a corporate training program?

6. **Random Word Association:** Pick a random word from a dictionary or a random image. Force yourself to connect that random word or image to your problem or area of interest. This seemingly arbitrary connection can spark unexpected insights and break you out of conventional thought patterns. For example, if your problem is "improving team collaboration" and your random word is "umbrella," you might think about how an umbrella protects everyone, leading to ideas about creating a "protective framework" for team communication.

Remember, the initial brainstorming phase is about maximizing quantity and embracing diversity. Defer all judgment. Capture everything, no matter how outlandish it seems at first glance. The critical evaluation and refinement will come later.

Identifying Your Unique Value

Once you have generated a robust pool of ideas, the next critical step is to begin the process of identifying and articulating their **unique value proposition (UVP)**. In a world saturated with options, where consumers and clients are constantly bombarded with choices, simply having an idea isn't enough; it needs to stand out, to offer something compellingly different and better. Your UVP is the single, clear statement that explains what makes your idea distinct and superior to the alternatives, and why a specific audience would choose it over others. It's not just a marketing slogan; it's the core promise of your idea.To effectively identify and refine your unique value, ask yourself the following rigorous questions:

- **What problem does this idea *truly* solve, and for whom?** Be incredibly specific. Don't just say "it helps people." What specific pain point, unmet need, desire, or challenge does it address for a clearly defined group of individuals or organizations? For example, instead of "It helps people exercise," specify "It helps busy professionals fit effective 15-minute workouts into their lunch breaks without needing a gym." The more precise you are about the problem and the audience, the clearer your value becomes.

- **Who is this idea *specifically* for? (Define your target audience clearly.)** An idea that tries to serve everyone often ends up serving no one well. Niche down. Who are your ideal users or customers? What are their demographics, psychographics, behaviors, and existing habits? Understanding your target audience deeply allows you to tailor your value proposition to their specific needs and desires, making your idea far more compelling and relevant. For instance, an idea for "sustainable clothing" is broad; an idea for "sustainable, ethically sourced activewear for female runners aged 25-40" is much more focused.

- **How is this idea genuinely different from what already exists in the market?** This is where you conduct a thorough, honest comparison with current solutions, competitors, or even the status quo (how people solve the problem without your idea). Does your idea offer a unique feature that no one else has? Does it provide a significantly better user experience, making it easier or more enjoyable to use? Is it offered at a lower cost, or does it deliver higher quality? Does it employ a novel approach or technology? Does it solve a problem that current solutions only partially address? Your differentiation could be in product, service, pricing, distribution, or even branding and community.

- **What is the core benefit, not just the features?** Beyond a list of features, what tangible or emotional benefit does your idea *truly* provide to the user? Does it save them time, save them money, reduce their stress, bring them joy, improve their health, enhance their status, or simplify their life? People buy benefits, not just features. For example, a feature might be "cloud storage," but the benefit is "peace of mind knowing your data is always safe and accessible from anywhere." Always translate features into the direct value they provide to the user.

- **Can it be easily copied, and what makes it defensible?** In a competitive landscape, your unique value needs to be sustainable. Consider what makes your idea difficult for others to replicate quickly or cheaply. Is it built on a unique process, proprietary technology (e.g., a patent, a unique algorithm), a strong and recognizable brand identity, a deeply specialized niche that requires specific expertise, a unique distribution channel, or strong network effects? While few ideas are truly uncopyable, building in layers of defensibility early on strengthens your long-term potential.

Your unique value proposition is not just a marketing slogan; it's the strategic heart of your idea. It guides your development process, helps you communicate its purpose clearly and compellingly to potential users, investors, and collaborators, and ultimately determines its potential for success and impact. Refining your UVP is an iterative process that involves a blend of introspection, rigorous market research, testing assumptions, and a willingness to be brutally honest about your idea's strengths, weaknesses, and competitive landscape.

Generating ideas is not a one-time event but an ongoing process, a continuous loop of keen observation, persistent questioning, and fearless creative exploration. By actively seeking the diverse origins of great ideas, employing a variety of powerful brainstorming techniques, and rigorously defining your unique value proposition, you transform vague inspirations into compelling, actionable concepts ready for development. This robust foundation will serve you well as you move forward. In the next chapter, we will delve into shaping your vision, giving even greater clarity and purpose to your most promising ideas, moving them closer to reality.

Chapter 6

Shaping Your Vision: Clarity and Purpose

In the previous chapter, you learned to become a prolific idea generator, unearthing potential solutions and identifying your unique value. You now likely have a rich collection of promising ideas, perhaps even a clear favorite among them that resonates deeply with your passions and skills. But an idea, no matter how brilliant, how innovative, or how deeply it addresses an unmet need, remains just a raw concept, a mere blueprint, until it is imbued with profound **clarity and unwavering purpose**. This chapter is about taking that raw, unrefined idea and transforming it into a compelling, actionable vision. It's about defining its essence, articulating its ultimate impact, and setting a precise, inspiring direction for its development. Without a crystal-clear vision, even the most innovative ideas can wander aimlessly, lose crucial momentum, become diluted by competing priorities, or simply fade away in the face of challenges.

Think of your idea as a nascent seed, full of dormant potential. Idea generation, as we discussed, was about finding that seed, perhaps even cultivating a small collection of them. Now, in this pivotal stage, we're going to define the magnificent, thriving tree it's destined to become – its species, its size, its purpose in the ecosystem. This involves answering fundamental, often challenging, questions that will serve as your unwavering guiding stars throughout the demanding yet immensely rewarding journey of bringing your idea to full fruition. This clarity will not only provide direction but also act as a powerful filter, helping you make decisions, allocate resources, and stay true to your core intent.

Defining Your "Why"

Before you can effectively articulate *what* your idea is (its features, its form) or *how* it will work (its processes, its mechanics), you must first understand its deepest, most fundamental **"why."** This isn't merely about the superficial motivations like making money, achieving fame, or gaining recognition, though these can be natural byproducts of success. Your "why" delves into the core motivation, the underlying problem you are truly passionate about solving, the profound impact you genuinely aspire to make in the world, or the fundamental human need you aim to fulfill. As the acclaimed author and speaker Simon Sinek famously articulated, "People don't buy what you do; they buy why you do it." Your "why" is the emotional and philosophical bedrock of your idea, providing meaning, direction, and an inexhaustible wellspring of resilience when obstacles inevitably arise and the path becomes difficult. It's the intrinsic fuel that keeps you going when external rewards seem distant.

To uncover your authentic "why," engage in a deep, honest self-inquiry. Ask yourself:

- **What problem truly bothers me or my target audience on a fundamental level?** Go beyond the surface-level inconvenience. Is it a systemic inefficiency that wastes precious resources? An injustice that marginalizes a community? A lack of access to vital information or services? A pervasive gap in human connection in an increasingly digital world? Or a fundamental inconvenience that drains joy from daily life? Dig into the emotional, social, or economic impact of this problem. Feel the pain point. For instance, if your idea is a new educational platform, is your "why" truly about democratizing knowledge, or is it merely about creating a profitable online course? The former is far more compelling and sustainable.

- **What specific, tangible change do I genuinely want to see in the world as a direct result of this idea's existence?** Envision the ideal future state your idea helps create. How will things be tangibly different, unequivocally better, or more fulfilling for your target audience and beyond? Will people be healthier, more connected, more informed, more efficient, or more empowered? Paint a vivid picture of this transformed reality. For a non-profit focused on clean water, the "why" isn't just "to provide water," but "to eradicate waterborne diseases and empower communities to thrive by ensuring universal access to clean, safe drinking water."

- **What core values does this idea represent for me, personally and professionally?** Does it align intrinsically with your personal ethics, your beliefs about community responsibility, environmental sustainability, fostering creativity, promoting empowerment, or championing transparency? When your idea is deeply rooted in your values, it feels authentic, purposeful, and inherently sustainable. It becomes an extension of who you are, making the work feel less like a chore and more like a calling. This alignment also makes it easier to attract like-minded collaborators and customers.

- **What would be the ultimate, far-reaching impact if this idea succeeded beyond my wildest dreams?** Allow yourself to dream big. Paint a vivid, expansive picture of the positive ripple effects your idea could generate. How would it change an industry, a community, or even the world? This helps connect your idea to a larger, more inspiring purpose, transcending its immediate form. For a new musical instrument, the ultimate impact might be "to unlock a new form of human expression that fosters global connection through sound."

- **Why *me*? Why am I uniquely positioned or the right person to bring this particular idea to life?** This question connects your unique skills, experiences, passions, and insights (as discussed in Chapter 5) directly to the problem you're solving and the vision you're pursuing. What specific combination of background, talent, and lived experience makes you uniquely suited to champion this idea? This isn't about ego; it's about acknowledging your authentic connection and leverage.

Your "why" should be concise, inspiring, and deeply personal – something you can articulate in a single, powerful sentence or two. It's the mission statement for your idea, the rallying cry that will motivate you through the darkest days and attract others to your cause. For example, if your idea is a sustainable clothing brand, your "why" might be "to empower consumers to dress ethically without compromising style, fostering a more sustainable and conscious fashion industry for a healthier planet." This "why" is far more powerful and motivating than simply "to sell clothes." It provides a clear, purpose-driven narrative that transcends the product itself, connecting with values and aspirations.

Setting Clear Goals for Your Idea

Once your "why" is firmly established, providing the overarching purpose and direction, the next essential step is to translate that inspiring vision into concrete, measurable goals. As the saying goes, "A vision without goals is merely a dream; goals without a vision are just tasks." This is the critical juncture where you define what tangible success looks like for your idea, not just in the distant future, but at various, manageable stages of its development. Without clear goals, your efforts can become scattered, resources can be wasted, and the risk of demotivation due to a lack of perceived progress increases dramatically.

Effective goals are universally understood to be **SMART**:

- **S - Specific:** Clearly and unambiguously define what you want to achieve. Avoid vague language. Instead of "I want to make a popular app," say "I want to develop a mobile app that helps users track their daily water intake and provides personalized hydration reminders." Specificity helps you focus your efforts and communicate your intent clearly to others. What exactly will be done? By whom? For whom?

- **M - Measurable:** How will you know if you've achieved your goal? Include quantifiable metrics that allow you to track progress and determine completion. "The app will achieve 1,000 active daily users within six months of launch," or "Secure $50,000 in seed funding," or "Reduce customer support response time by 20%." Measurable goals provide objective benchmarks for success and allow for data-driven adjustments.

- **A - Achievable (but challenging):** While your goals should push you beyond your comfort zone, they must also be realistic given your current resources, skills, and market conditions. Don't set yourself up for immediate, demoralizing failure. An achievable goal is one you can realistically accomplish with effort and strategic planning. This doesn't mean easy; it means possible. For instance, launching a global social network in three months with no funding is likely unachievable, but launching a local beta version might be.

- **R - Relevant:** Ensure your goals align directly with your "why" and the overall vision for your idea. Is this particular goal truly important to the success and purpose of your idea? Does it contribute meaningfully to the bigger picture? Pursuing irrelevant goals, no matter how well-defined, can lead to wasted effort and a diversion from your core mission. Every goal should serve the overarching "why."

- **T - Time-bound:** Set a clear deadline or timeframe for each goal. This creates a sense of urgency, provides a framework for accountability, and helps you prioritize tasks. "Launch the beta version of the app by Q4 this year," or "Complete the first draft of

the business plan by the end of next month."
Deadlines prevent procrastination and encourage
focused action.

Beyond a single overarching goal, consider setting a
hierarchy of goals that cascade from your grand vision
down to daily tasks:

- **Visionary Goal:** This is the ultimate, long-term
  impact or aspiration of your idea, directly aligned
  with your "why." (e.g., "To revolutionize personal
  wellness through accessible, intuitive technology
  that empowers individuals to take control of their
  health journeys"). This is your North Star.

- **Strategic Goals:** These are major milestones that
  represent significant progress towards your
  visionary goal, typically spanning months or even a
  year or two. (e.g., "Achieve market validation for the
  core concept," "Secure initial seed funding," "Build a
  core user base of 10,000 engaged users," "Establish
  key partnerships"). These are the major waypoints on
  your journey.

- **Tactical Goals:** These are shorter-term, highly
  actionable steps that directly contribute to achieving
  your strategic goals, often spanning weeks or days.
  (e.g., "Conduct 20 user interviews to validate
  problem," "Develop a clickable prototype of the app's
  main features," "Create a compelling pitch deck for

potential investors," "Research competitor pricing models"). These are the specific actions you take to move forward.

Regularly reviewing and adjusting your goals is crucial. The world is dynamic, and as your idea evolves, as you gather more information, and as market conditions shift, your goals may need to adapt. This isn't a sign of failure or weakness, but rather of intelligent responsiveness, agility, and a commitment to continuous learning. Treat your goals as living documents, subject to refinement based on new insights.

Visualizing Success

With your "why" deeply defined and your goals precisely set, the final, incredibly powerful step in shaping your vision is to **visualize success**. This isn't just a passive, feel-good exercise or a New Age fad; it's a scientifically proven psychological technique that primes your brain for achievement, enhances motivation, and helps you identify potential steps or obstacles more clearly. When you vividly imagine your desired outcome, your brain activates many of the same neural pathways that would fire if you were actually experiencing it. This mental rehearsal strengthens your belief in your ability to achieve the goal, boosts confidence, and can even help you subconsciously identify necessary actions or solutions.

How to effectively engage in this powerful practice of visualizing success:

1. **Create a Detailed Mental Movie:** Dedicate a few quiet minutes each day to this practice. Close your eyes and imagine your idea fully realized in exquisite detail. What does it look like, feel like, sound like? Who is using it, and how are they benefiting? What specific problems has it solved? What emotions are you feeling as you witness its success – pride, joy, fulfillment, relief? Engage all your senses: If it's a physical product, imagine holding it, feeling its texture, seeing its design, hearing its operational sounds. If it's a service, imagine the positive interactions, the testimonials, the transformed lives. Make it as real and immersive as possible.

2. **Focus on the Process, Not Just the Outcome:** While visualizing the glorious end result is important for motivation, also spend significant time visualizing yourself *engaging in the actions* that lead to that success. See yourself overcoming challenges with grace, learning new skills with enthusiasm, collaborating effectively with others, persevering through setbacks, and making smart decisions. This "process visualization" is crucial because it builds confidence not just in the *result*, but in your *ability to navigate the journey*. It mentally rehearses the effort and problem-solving required, making the path feel more achievable and less daunting.

3. **Use Affirmations and Mantras:** Pair your visualization practice with positive affirmations and empowering mantras that reinforce your belief in the vision and your capacity to achieve it. As you visualize, repeat phrases like: "My idea is creating significant positive impact and transforming lives," or "I am effectively bringing my vision to life with clarity and purpose," or "Every action I take moves me closer to my desired outcome." These statements, when combined with vivid imagery, can deeply embed the desired beliefs into your subconscious.

4. **Create a Vision Board:** A physical or digital collage of images, words, quotes, and symbols that visually represent your idea's success, your "why," and the lifestyle or impact you desire. This serves as a tangible, constant reminder and a powerful source of inspiration. Place it where you'll see it daily – near your workspace, on your phone background, or as your computer desktop. The visual cues reinforce your vision and keep it top-of-mind, subconsciously guiding your decisions throughout the day.

5. **Regular and Consistent Practice:** Like any mental muscle, visualization strengthens with consistent use. Dedicate a few minutes each day, ideally at the start or end of your day, to this visualization practice. Consistency is key to embedding the vision deeply in your subconscious mind, making it feel

more real and attainable. The more you practice, the more your brain will begin to seek out and recognize opportunities that align with your visualized future.

Shaping your vision is an act of profound intentional creation. It's about taking the raw potential of an idea and giving it precise form, compelling meaning, and an unshakeable direction. By deeply understanding your "why," setting clear, measurable, and actionable SMART goals, and vividly visualizing success (both outcome and process), you transform a mere concept into a powerful, actionable blueprint for impact. This newfound clarity will serve as your unwavering compass, guiding every decision, prioritizing every action, and sustaining your motivation as you move into the next crucial phase: the iterative journey of prototyping and testing, where your vision begins to take physical form.

Chapter 7

The Iterative Journey: Prototyping and Testing

You've successfully defined your "why," meticulously set clear, actionable goals, and vividly visualized the triumphant success of your idea. Your vision is now a powerful, illuminating beacon, steadfastly guiding your path forward. However, a vision, no matter how compelling, how inspiring, or how meticulously crafted, remains an abstract concept, a beautiful dream, until it begins to take tangible, physical form. This chapter marks a crucial and exhilarating shift from the realm of pure conceptualization and strategic planning to the dynamic world of action and real-world interaction: **the iterative journey of prototyping and testing**. This is the vital stage where your idea moves from the confines of your mind and your planning documents into the hands of real people, allowing you to learn, refine, and adapt based on actual interaction, honest observation, and invaluable feedback.

The word "iterative" is not just a buzzword here; it is the fundamental principle that underpins all successful innovation and growth. It means a continuous, cyclical process of repeating, refining, and improving. You will rarely, if ever, build the perfect solution on your very first attempt – no one truly does. Instead, you'll create rough, imperfect versions (prototypes), test them rigorously with your target audience, learn deeply from the results (both successes and failures), and then refine your idea, repeating this cycle again and again. This disciplined, iterative approach is a powerful antidote to risk, as it minimizes upfront investment, conserves precious resources (time, money, energy), and, most importantly, dramatically accelerates your learning curve, ensuring your idea evolves in the right direction. It's the engine of progress, allowing you to build momentum and confidence through continuous, validated learning.

Embracing Imperfection

One of the most significant and often insidious hurdles for aspiring idea-growers is the relentless, often subconscious, pursuit of perfection. The inner critic, which we learned to acknowledge and reframe in Chapter 4, frequently whispers insidious doubts: "Your idea isn't ready yet," "It needs more features," "It requires more polish," or "You need more time before it can possibly be shown to anyone." This insidious perfectionism is a silent, yet potent, killer of brilliant ideas. It leads to endless delays, paralyzing analysis, wasted effort on unnecessary or unvalidated features, and, most tragically, results in countless potentially transformative ideas that never see the light of day, remaining forever trapped in the realm of "almost." This fear of imperfection often stems from a fear of judgment, a desire for external validation, or an ego that struggles with the idea of presenting anything less than flawless.

Embracing imperfection means fundamentally understanding and accepting that your first version, your initial prototype, or your very first attempt will be flawed. It will be rough, it will be incomplete, and it will likely have bugs or awkward elements. And that's not just okay; it's **absolutely essential** for genuine progress. Think of it as a sculptor's first rough block of marble – it bears little resemblance to the final, polished masterpiece, but it is the absolutely necessary starting point, the raw material from which the final form will emerge through successive refinements. This principle is often encapsulated in the Silicon Valley mantra: "If you're not embarrassed by the first version of your product, you've launched too late." This isn't about advocating for sloppiness, but for strategic humility and a focus on core functionality for learning.

Here's a deeper dive into why embracing imperfection is vital for your idea's growth:

- **Speed to Learning is Paramount:** In the dynamic landscape of ideas, the fastest way to learn if your core assumption has merit, if your solution truly addresses a problem, and if your audience genuinely desires it, is to put a rough, functional version of it in front of real people as quickly as possible. You can spend months, even years, theorizing, planning, and debating internally, but nothing, absolutely nothing, beats the immediate, unfiltered data and insights gained from actual user interaction. An imperfect prototype provides invaluable, actionable data that theoretical analysis simply cannot. It allows you to fail fast, learn faster, and adapt with agility, pivoting your idea based on real-world evidence rather than mere speculation. This rapid feedback loop is what separates successful innovators from those who remain stuck in endless planning.

- **Resource Conservation and Risk Mitigation:** Building a perfect, fully-featured product or service from the outset, based purely on assumptions, is an incredibly expensive and high-risk endeavor in terms of time, money, and emotional energy. An imperfect prototype, often referred to as a **Minimum Viable Product (MVP)**, allows you to test your core assumptions with the absolute minimal investment required to get meaningful feedback. The MVP is not about building a shoddy product; it's about building the *smallest possible thing* that delivers core value and allows you to learn. This strategic frugality prevents you from sinking vast resources into an idea that might not resonate with your target market, or that needs fundamental changes. It's about de-risking your venture step by step, making small, informed bets rather than one huge, blind leap. For example, before building a complex online course platform, an

MVP might be delivering the course content manually via email to a small group to validate demand and content effectiveness.

- **Validation, Not Perfection, is the Early Goal:** The primary objective of early prototypes and MVPs is not to achieve a flawless product, but to **validate your core assumptions**. Do people actually experience the problem you're trying to solve? Is that problem significant enough for them to seek a solution? Does your proposed solution actually help them alleviate that problem effectively? Are they willing to use it, and perhaps even pay for it? These are the critical questions that imperfect prototypes help you answer. They are tools for learning, for proving or disproving hypotheses about your market and solution, not finished products for sale.

  This distinction is crucial for maintaining focus and preventing feature creep – the tendency to add more and more features before validating the core concept, leading to bloated, unfocused offerings.

- **Overcoming Analysis Paralysis and Building Momentum:** The fear of not being perfect, combined with the sheer complexity and unknown variables of a new idea, often leads to analysis paralysis. This is a state where you get stuck in endless planning, exhaustive research, and theoretical refinement without ever taking concrete action. Embracing imperfection is the direct antidote; it forces you to take action, even small, seemingly insignificant ones. Each imperfect prototype you create and test builds tangible momentum, generates visible progress, and provides a sense of accomplishment, which in turn fuels further action and significantly reduces the psychological burden of starting. It transforms the daunting task of "building a great idea" into a series of manageable, learnable steps.

Your initial prototype doesn't need to be a polished masterpiece. Its form should be dictated by the specific assumption you want to test and the quickest, cheapest way to test it.

It could be as simple as:

- A **sketch on a napkin** demonstrating a user flow for an app, showing how a user would move from one screen to another.
- A **simple flowchart** outlining a new service process, detailing each step a customer would take and what happens at each stage.
- A **PowerPoint presentation or a series of static mock-up screens** simulating the interactive experience of an app or website, clicking through slides to mimic navigation.
- A **basic landing page** describing your proposed service or product, with a clear call to action (e.g.,

"Learn More," "Sign Up for Early Access," "Pre-order Now") to gauge genuine interest before building anything.

- A **"Wizard of Oz" MVP**, where you manually perform tasks that a future automated system would handle. For example, if you're building an AI-powered personal assistant, you might initially *be* the assistant, manually responding to user requests to understand their needs and test the value proposition.
- Even just a **structured conversation** where you meticulously explain your idea to someone from your target audience and gauge their detailed reaction, asking specific questions about their pain points, their current solutions, and their potential interest in your proposed solution.

The simpler, the better, as long as it allows you to test a key assumption about your idea's viability, desirability, or feasibility. The goal is to get *something* in front of users quickly to learn.

Gathering Feedback and Learning

Once you have an imperfect prototype, the next crucial and continuous step is to put it in front of your target audience and **gather feedback**. This is where the real, often surprising, and sometimes uncomfortable, learning happens. It's the moment of truth where your assumptions meet reality, and where your internal vision is confronted with external perspectives. However, not all feedback is created equal, and knowing how to collect, interpret, and act upon it effectively is both an art and a science that requires a disciplined approach.

Here's how to approach feedback with a growth mindset and maximize your learning:

1. **Seek Out Your *Actual* Target Audience:** This is non-negotiable. Do not fall into the trap of only asking friends, family, or colleagues unless they are genuinely representative of your defined target audience (as meticulously identified in Chapter 5). Their well-meaning but unqualified opinions can lead you significantly astray. Instead, actively seek out people who actually experience the problem your idea aims to solve, or who would genuinely use and benefit from your solution. Recruit participants through online forums, social media groups, industry events, professional networks, or even by approaching people in relevant real-world settings (e.g., a coffee shop if your idea is for remote workers). Their insights will be the most valuable, actionable, and representative of real market needs.

2. **Ask Open-Ended, Behavior-Focused Questions:** Avoid leading questions or those that elicit simple "yes/no" answers, which provide minimal insight. Instead of "Do you like it?" (which is subjective and unhelpful), ask questions that encourage detailed

responses about their experience, their needs, their current behaviors, and their thought processes. Examples:

- "Walk me through how you would use this (prototype/idea) in your daily life, step by step." (This reveals actual usage patterns.)
- "What problems, if any, does this solve for you that you currently face?" (Focus on problem validation.)
- "What did you find confusing, frustrating, or difficult about this experience?" (Identify friction points.)
- "If this were available today, what specific features or aspects would make it indispensable for you?" (Uncover core value drivers.)
- "How does this compare to how you currently solve this problem, or what alternatives do you use?" (Understand competitive landscape from their perspective.)
- "What emotions did you experience while interacting with this, and why?" (Tap into deeper motivations and frustrations.) Focus on understanding their underlying needs, motivations, and existing behaviors, not just their opinion on your specific solution. The "why" behind their answers is often more important than the "what."

3. **Observe Behavior, Not Just Words:** This is a critical distinction. People often say one thing and do another, or they might struggle to articulate their true needs or frustrations. If possible, observe how users actually interact with your prototype. Do they struggle with certain features even if they verbally say they "understand" them? Do they hesitate at specific points? Do they use it in unexpected ways that reveal an unaddressed need? Do they abandon a task midway? Their actions, their body language, their points of friction, and their workarounds often speak louder and more truthfully than their words. For example, a user might *say* they love a particular feature, but if you observe them consistently skipping it or struggling to find it, their behavior tells a different story about its true utility or discoverability. Record these observations diligently.

4. **Listen Actively, Without Defensiveness:** This is perhaps the hardest, yet most critical, part of gathering feedback, especially when the feedback is critical. Your idea is your "baby," and criticism can feel deeply personal, triggering your inner critic and ego. Practice active listening (revisit Chapter 3's "Beginner's Mind" for this principle of open receptivity). Resist the overwhelming urge to explain, justify, defend your choices, or "educate" the user on why they're wrong or why your design makes sense. Your sole goal in this moment is to understand their perspective, their pain points, and

their genuine experience, not to convince them. Thank them sincerely for their honesty and their time, even if the feedback is difficult to hear. Remember, they are helping you improve your idea and avoid costly mistakes down the line; they are not judging you as a person. This ability to detach emotionally from the feedback is a hallmark of truly resilient and growth-oriented creators.

5. **Look for Patterns, Not Isolated Comments:** One person's feedback might be an anomaly, a unique preference, or a misunderstanding specific to them. It's important to listen to every piece of feedback, but don't overreact to single comments. However, if three or more people independently highlight the same issue, express the same desire, or struggle with the same part of your prototype, that's a strong, reliable signal that warrants serious attention. Prioritize feedback that reveals recurring patterns and addresses core problems or significantly enhances the unique value proposition you defined in Chapter 5. Don't get distracted by every single suggestion or minor aesthetic preference; focus on the insights that affect the most users or the most critical aspects of your idea's functionality and value.

6. **Categorize and Prioritize Feedback Systematically:** After gathering a significant amount of feedback, organize it in a structured, objective way. Create

clear themes or categories (e.g., "Usability Issues," "Missing Core Features," "Value Proposition Confusion," "Performance Bugs," "Positive Feedback/Delighters," "Feature Requests"). Then, prioritize the changes based on their potential impact versus the effort required to implement them.

A useful framework for this is the **Impact/Effort Matrix:**

- **High Impact, Low Effort (Quick Wins):** Tackle these first. They provide significant value or solve critical problems with minimal investment.
- **High Impact, High Effort (Strategic Initiatives):** Plan these strategically. These are often crucial for long-term success but require more resources and careful planning.
- **Low Impact, Low Effort (Nice-to-Haves):** Consider these if time and resources allow, but don't prioritize them over high-impact items.
- **Low Impact, High Effort (Avoid):** These are resource drains with little return on investment. Avoid them unless absolutely necessary. This systematic approach ensures you're making data-driven decisions about your next iteration, focusing your efforts where they will yield the greatest return.

Feedback is not a judgment; it is a precious gift. It's the raw data that helps you refine your idea, steer it towards true market fit, and ensure it solves a real problem for real people in a way they genuinely value. It's not a reflection on your worth, but an invaluable guide for your next iteration, a compass helping you navigate the complex terrain of innovation.

The Power of Small Experiments

The entire iterative journey is powered by the philosophy of **small experiments**. Instead of betting everything on one grand, all-or-nothing launch, which carries immense risk and potential for catastrophic failure, you strategically break down your idea into its core assumptions, formulate them as testable hypotheses, and then run small, low-risk experiments to validate or invalidate those hypotheses. Each experiment is a focused learning opportunity, akin to a scientific inquiry, providing concrete data that informs your next steps and systematically reduces uncertainty. This approach embodies the "build-measure-learn" loop: build a minimal prototype, measure its performance and user reaction, and learn from the data to inform the next iteration.

Examples of diverse small experiments to test various aspects of your idea:

- **Problem Validation Experiment (User Interviews & Surveys):** Before building anything tangible, conduct in-depth, unbiased interviews with 10-20 people from your target audience. Supplement this with surveys distributed to a larger group. The hypothesis: "We believe [Target Audience] experiences [Specific Problem] acutely, leading to [Negative Consequence], and they are actively looking for a solution." The metric: Number of interviewees who strongly confirm the problem and its severity; survey response rates and qualitative feedback. Decision rule: If less than 70% of interviewees confirm the problem's significance, or survey data is weak, re-evaluate the problem or target audience before proceeding.

- **Solution Validation Experiment (Landing Page/Smoke Test):** Create a simple, compelling landing page describing your proposed solution and its benefits, with a clear call to action (e.g., "Sign up for early access," "Pre-order now," "Join the waitlist"). Drive a small, targeted amount of traffic to it (e.g., via social media ads, targeted online communities). The hypothesis: "We believe [Target Audience] is interested enough in [Proposed Solution] to provide their contact information, indicating genuine demand." The metric: Conversion rate (percentage of visitors who sign up/pre-order). Decision rule: If conversion is below a predefined threshold (e.g., 5%), the solution or messaging needs significant refinement; if above, proceed to build a basic functional prototype.

- **Feature Test (A/B Testing or Usability Testing):** If you have two different ideas for a specific feature (e.g., two different button designs, two different headlines, two different onboarding flows), create two versions of your prototype or landing page. Show one version (A) to half your users and the other (B) to the other half (A/B testing). Alternatively, conduct one-on-one usability tests where users attempt specific tasks with your prototype. The hypothesis: "We believe Feature A will result in higher engagement/task completion than Feature B." The metric: Click-through rate, time on page, task completion rate, error rate. Decision rule: Implement the version that performs better based on the chosen metric.

- **Concierge MVP (Manual Service Delivery):** Instead of building a complex automated system, manually perform the core service for a small group of early users. This allows you to test the fundamental value proposition and user experience without significant technical investment. The hypothesis: "We believe users will value [core service] enough to pay for it, even if delivered manually and imperfectly." The metric: Number of paying customers, customer satisfaction scores, qualitative feedback on the manual process. Example: Dropbox initially tested demand for their file-syncing service with a simple video explaining the concept, rather than building the full software, to gauge interest.

- **Pricing Test (Tiered Offers or Surveys):** Offer your service or product at different price points to different segments of your target audience (e.g., through different landing pages, segmented email offers, or direct conversations). Alternatively, conduct surveys asking about willingness to pay for specific features. The hypothesis: "We believe [Target Audience] is willing to pay [Price X] for [Value Proposition], and this price point will maximize revenue while maintaining demand." The metric: Conversion rate at each price point, average revenue per user, customer acquisition cost. Decision rule: Identify the optimal price point that balances demand, perceived value, and profitability.

- **Crowdfunding Campaign (Market Validation & Funding):** Launching a crowdfunding campaign (e.g., Kickstarter, Indiegogo) can serve as a powerful experiment. The hypothesis: "We believe there is sufficient market demand for [Product/Idea] at [Price Point] to attract a critical mass of early adopters." The metric: Amount of funds raised, number of backers, speed of funding. Decision rule: If the campaign meets its goal, it validates demand and provides initial funding; if not, it signals a need to re-evaluate the idea, pricing, or marketing.

Each small experiment should be meticulously designed with:

- **A Clear, Testable Hypothesis:** This is your assumption stated as a belief that can be proven or disproven. (e.g., "We believe busy parents will pay for a meal planning service that saves them 3 hours a week.")

- **A Defined, Quantifiable Metric:** How will you objectively measure success or failure? This must be specific and unambiguous. (e.g., "We will consider the experiment successful if 10% of landing page visitors sign up for the paid service within 2 weeks.")

- **A Realistic Timeframe:** When will the experiment run, and for how long? This ensures focus and prevents endless testing. (e.g., "The experiment will run for 7 days, from Monday to Sunday.")

- **A Clear Decision Rule:** What will you do based on the results? This prevents ambiguity and ensures action. (e.g., "If sign-ups are below 5%, we'll re-evaluate the problem or solution; if above 10%, we'll proceed to build a basic functional prototype; if between 5% and 10%, we'll iterate on the landing page and run another test.")

The profound power of small experiments lies in their ability to rapidly de-risk your idea. You are empowered to "fail fast," learn quickly from those failures, and "pivot cheaply" before significant resources are committed. This agile, data-driven approach prevents you from investing heavily in an idea that no one truly wants or needs, and instead systematically guides you towards a solution that truly resonates with your target market and fulfills your vision. It's about moving from untested assumptions to validated knowledge, one small, deliberate, and intelligent step at a time. This continuous cycle of build-measure-learn is the engine of sustainable growth and ensures that your idea is consistently evolving towards greater impact and viability.

The iterative journey of prototyping and testing is not a one-time phase but a continuous loop of creation, observation, learning, and refinement. By embracing imperfection as a virtue, actively seeking and intelligently interpreting feedback, and running small, focused experiments, you transform your idea from a theoretical concept into a robust, market-validated solution. This hands-on, evidence-based approach builds immense confidence, accelerates your learning curve exponentially, and ensures that your idea is truly growing in the direction of maximum impact and viability. In the next chapter, we will delve deeper into the crucial skills of overcoming obstacles and effective problem-solving for sustained growth, which are indispensable companions to the iterative process.

Chapter 8

Overcoming Obstacles: Problem-Solving for Growth

You've diligently embraced the iterative journey, prototyping your ideas, gathering invaluable feedback, and refining your concept based on real-world interactions. This hands-on, data-driven approach is specifically designed to accelerate learning and hone your idea into something truly impactful. However, even with the most diligent planning, the most insightful testing, and the most robust prototypes, the path to growing your ideas is rarely, if ever, smooth, linear, or free of friction. Obstacles are not unfortunate exceptions or random occurrences; they are an inherent, unavoidable, and indeed, essential part of the process of innovation and growth. Every significant achievement is punctuated by moments of challenge, confusion, and potential failure. This chapter is dedicated to equipping you with not just the right mindset, but also the practical strategies and tools for effectively **overcoming obstacles and mastering problem-solving for sustained growth.** It's about transforming stumbling blocks into stepping stones, and setbacks into opportunities for deeper learning and stronger solutions.

Remember, as we discussed in Chapter 2, true optimism isn't about ignoring problems, pretending they don't exist, or living in a state of naive denial. Instead, it's about perceiving them as opportunities – invitations to innovate, to learn, to adapt, and to strengthen your resolve. This chapter will delve into how to apply that principle directly and systematically to the myriad challenges you will inevitably face as you nurture your ideas from concept to reality.

Anticipating Challenges

Many people are caught entirely off guard by obstacles, viewing them as unfortunate surprises, unexpected bad luck, or random misfortunes that inexplicably derail progress. This reactive stance often leads to panic, hasty decisions, and a sense of being overwhelmed. However, a proactive growth mindset understands that challenges are not only predictable but, in many cases, can be reasonably anticipated. By consciously anticipating potential hurdles, you can mentally prepare, develop robust contingency plans, and even proactively mitigate significant risks before they fully materialize, thereby reducing their impact or preventing them altogether. This isn't about dwelling on negativity or inviting problems; it's about strategic foresight, intelligent preparation, and building resilience into your process from the outset. It's about playing chess, not checkers, with your idea's future.

Think of it like a seasoned traveler packing for a complex, multi-destination journey. They don't just pack for sunshine and smooth sailing; they meticulously consider the possibility of rain, unexpected flight delays, lost luggage, cultural misunderstandings, and potential detours. They pack a versatile wardrobe, backup chargers, copies of important documents, and a flexible itinerary. Similarly, for your idea, it's crucial to systematically consider the various categories of challenges that might arise at different stages of its development and implementation:

1. **Technical Hurdles:** If your idea involves any form of technology (a website, an app, a physical product with electronic components, a complex algorithm), anticipate a wide array of technical difficulties. What if a key piece of software or a specific API doesn't integrate seamlessly as planned, causing unexpected compatibility issues? What if your website or application experiences critical bugs, leading to crashes or poor performance under heavy user traffic, especially during peak periods? What if scaling your solution to accommodate a larger user base proves far more complex or expensive than initially estimated? What if a critical third-party service you rely on changes its policies or shuts down? Proactive steps might include robust testing, building in redundancies, and having a clear plan for technical support and maintenance.

2. **Market/User Challenges:** Even if your initial user research was thorough, market dynamics and user needs are constantly evolving. What if your target audience doesn't respond as expected to your

solution, finding it confusing, unnecessary, or simply unappealing? What if their needs or preferences fundamentally evolve after you've built your solution, rendering it less relevant? What if a well-funded competitor suddenly launches a strikingly similar product or service, potentially with more resources or a stronger brand? What if your initial marketing message isn't resonating with your audience, failing to communicate your unique value proposition effectively? Anticipation here involves continuous market research, competitive analysis, and a willingness to iterate on your messaging and product features based on real-time feedback.

3. **Resource Constraints:** The availability of resources – time, money, and skilled personnel – is a perennial challenge for any new idea. Will you truly have enough runway (financial resources) to execute your vision through all its phases? What if a crucial funding round falls through, or unexpected expenses deplete your budget faster than anticipated? What if a key team member, whose expertise is indispensable, unexpectedly leaves the project? What if you struggle to attract the right talent or secure necessary partnerships? Proactive measures include building a financial buffer, having backup plans for key personnel, and diversifying your funding sources.

4. **Personal/Mindset Obstacles:** Even with the extensive work you've done on your mindset in Part 1 of this book, the journey of growing an idea is inherently stressful, and self-doubt can creep back in. What if you lose motivation after a series of setbacks, feeling discouraged or burnt out? What if you face significant personal setbacks (health issues, family emergencies) that demand your attention away from your idea? What if the sheer weight of responsibility or the pressure of expectations leads to decision paralysis or anxiety? Anticipating these internal challenges allows you to build in self-care routines, seek emotional support from your network, and proactively manage your energy levels.

5. **External Factors:** The broader environment can present unforeseen challenges that are entirely outside your control. Economic downturns can shrink markets and reduce consumer spending. New regulatory changes or government policies can impact your ability to operate or even render your idea illegal. Unforeseen global events (like pandemics or natural disasters) can fundamentally shift consumer behavior, supply chains, or market priorities. Geopolitical instability can affect international operations. While these are harder to predict with precision, having a flexible strategy and diversified approach can help mitigate their impact.

To anticipate effectively, engage in a powerful "pre-mortem" exercise, a technique often used in project management. Instead of waiting for failure to happen and then analyzing it (a post-mortem), imagine your idea has failed catastrophically a year from now. Gather your team (or just yourself, if working solo) and ask: "It's a year from now, and our idea has completely failed. What went wrong? What were all the reasons for this failure?" Work backward from that imagined failure to identify all the potential causes, both internal and external. This inverse thinking can reveal risks and vulnerabilities you might otherwise overlook because your brain is wired to focus on success. For each potential challenge identified in this pre-mortem, ask:

- What is the likelihood of this happening (High, Medium, Low)?
- What would be the impact if it did happen (Catastrophic, Significant, Minor)?
- What proactive steps can I take *now* to reduce its likelihood or severity? (e.g., "If funding falls through, we will have identified 3 alternative grant programs.")
- What would be my immediate response if it occurred? (e.g., "If the website crashes, we have a backup server ready to deploy within 15 minutes.")

This exercise transforms potential threats into manageable scenarios, allowing you to develop a strategic, proactive approach rather than reacting in crisis mode when problems inevitably strike. It builds a mental muscle for problem-solving before the pressure is on.

Creative Solutions and Adaptability

Once an obstacle inevitably presents itself, the ability to generate **creative solutions** and demonstrate unwavering **adaptability** becomes paramount. A fixed mindset, when confronted with a problem, might see it as a dead end, a reason to give up, or an insurmountable barrier. However, a growth mindset, fueled by curiosity and resilience, sees every problem as an invitation to innovate, a puzzle to be solved, or a challenge that will ultimately lead to a stronger, more refined idea. This requires a fundamental shift from a reactive "Oh no, this is impossible!" to a proactive, inquisitive "How might we overcome this?" or "What new possibilities does this challenge unlock?"

Here are comprehensive strategies for fostering creative problem-solving and cultivating deep adaptability:

1. **Reframe the Problem:** Often, the way we initially frame a problem limits our ability to find novel solutions. If your immediate thought is, "We don't have enough budget to build this feature," reframe it as, "How can we achieve the same impact with fewer resources?" or "What's the simplest, cheapest version of this feature that still delivers core value?" or "How can we find alternative funding sources or partners to build this?" A change in perspective, moving from

a deficit mindset to an abundance or possibility mindset, can unlock entirely new avenues for solutions. For example, the problem of "not enough parking" could be reframed as "how can we reduce the need for parking?" leading to ideas like better public transport or remote work.

2. **Brainstorm Diverse Solutions (Quantity over Quality, Again!):** When faced with an obstacle, resist the urge to jump to the first obvious solution. Instead, apply the powerful brainstorming techniques from Chapter 5 (Free Association, Mind Mapping, SCAMPER, Worst Idea Brainstorming, Role Storming) directly to the obstacle itself. Generate as many potential solutions as possible, no matter how outlandish, impractical, or seemingly silly they appear at first. The initial goal is sheer volume, not immediate feasibility. Encourage wild ideas, as they often contain the seeds of truly innovative, practical solutions. For instance, if a supply chain issue arises, brainstorm everything from "build our own factory" to "collaborate with a competitor" to "change the product design to use different materials."

3. **Break Down Complex Problems:** Large, monolithic obstacles can feel incredibly overwhelming and paralyzing. The key is to break them down into smaller, more manageable, and less intimidating components. For example, if the problem is "our product isn't selling," break it down into: "Is it a

marketing problem? A pricing problem? A product-market fit problem? A distribution problem?" Each smaller component then becomes a mini-problem to solve. Solving a series of small, discrete problems is far less daunting than tackling one giant, amorphous one. This also allows for incremental progress, builds confidence, and creates positive momentum.

4. **Seek Outside Perspectives and Diverse Input:** Your own perspective, no matter how brilliant, is inherently limited by your unique experiences, knowledge, and biases. When faced with a stubborn obstacle, actively consult with mentors, peers, experts from different fields, or even your target users. They might offer fresh insights, alternative strategies, or connections you hadn't considered. Sometimes, simply articulating your problem aloud to someone else can help you clarify your own thinking and spark a solution within yourself. Diverse teams, composed of individuals with varied backgrounds and thinking styles, consistently outperform homogenous teams in complex problem-solving scenarios. Actively solicit different viewpoints.

5. **Embrace Constraints as Catalysts for Creativity:** This is a counterintuitive but incredibly powerful strategy. Limitations – whether a tight budget, limited time, specific material restrictions, or

regulatory hurdles – can actually force innovative thinking. When resources are abundant, we often default to conventional, often expensive, solutions. When constraints are imposed, we are forced to think outside the box, challenge assumptions, and find novel, often more efficient, and resource-effective ways to achieve our goals. For example, the early days of Twitter were constrained by SMS message limits, forcing them to innovate with short-form communication. This constraint ultimately defined the platform's unique value. View constraints not as barriers, but as creative prompts.

6. **Learn from Adjacent Industries/Fields (Analogical Thinking):** Don't limit your search for solutions to your own industry or domain. Look for how similar problems are solved in entirely different domains. A logistics challenge in your business might find a creative solution inspired by how a hospital manages patient flow, how a theater company stages a complex production, or how a beehive efficiently organizes its workers. This "cross-pollination" or analogical thinking is a powerful source of innovation, as it allows you to transfer proven solutions from one context to another. Read widely, observe broadly, and make a habit of asking, "How would they solve this in [different industry]?"

7. **Cultivate a "Test and Learn" Approach to Solutions:** Don't expect your first proposed solution to an

obstacle to be perfect or to work flawlessly. Just as you prototype and test your main idea, treat each potential solution to a problem as a small experiment. Implement the most promising one on a small scale, measure its effectiveness with clear metrics, and learn from the results. If it doesn't work as intended, adapt, iterate, and try another approach. This iterative approach to problem-solving mirrors the prototyping process discussed in Chapter 7 and prevents you from committing too heavily to a single, unproven solution. It fosters agility and continuous improvement.

Adaptability is the profound willingness to change your approach, your strategy, or even your idea itself in response to new information, unforeseen circumstances, or validated feedback. It's about being flexible, agile, and responsive, rather than rigid, resistant, or stubbornly clinging to an original plan that no longer serves the evolving reality.

When to Pivot, When to Persist

Perhaps the most challenging and emotionally taxing decision in the face of significant obstacles is knowing when to **pivot** (make a fundamental, significant strategic change to your idea, business model, target market, or core technology) and when to **persist** (continue on your current path, perhaps with minor adjustments and refinements). This decision often comes down to distinguishing between a temporary setback that can be overcome with effort and a fundamental flaw in your core assumptions that demands a new direction. It requires a delicate balance of tenacity and humility.

Persist when:

- **The problem is solvable with effort and learning, and it's not a core invalidation:** The obstacle is a technical bug that can be fixed, a temporary resource constraint that can be overcome with creative fundraising, or a challenge that can be resolved by acquiring new skills, refining your existing approach, or improving execution. It's a bump in the road, not a broken bridge.

- **Your core "why" and unique value proposition remain strong and validated:** The market still demonstrably needs what you're offering, and your solution still addresses a real, significant problem for your target audience, even if the execution or initial delivery needs substantial work. You've confirmed the demand and the value.

- **Feedback indicates refinement, not reinvention:** Users are generally positive about the core concept but point to specific areas for improvement, feature enhancements, or usability fixes. They are not indicating a fundamental lack of interest in the core idea itself. The feedback is about *how* you deliver, not *what* you deliver.

- **You haven't fully tested your critical assumptions:**
  You might be hitting an obstacle because you haven't
  yet fully validated a critical hypothesis about your
  market, your solution, or your business model. In
  this case, persist in designing and running more
  focused experiments to test that specific hypothesis.
  Don't give up on the idea until you've gathered
  conclusive data.

Pivot when:

- **Your core assumptions are consistently and
  repeatedly invalidated by data:** Despite multiple
  iterations, experiments, and adjustments, users are
  consistently not engaging, not paying, or not finding
  significant value in your core solution. The market is
  simply not responding to your offering, or your
  initial problem hypothesis proves to be incorrect or
  not painful enough. This is the clearest signal for a
  pivot.
- **The problem you're solving isn't significant enough
  or doesn't truly exist:** You discover through
  extensive testing that while the problem might exist,
  it's not painful enough for people to actively seek or
  pay for a solution. Or, perhaps, your initial
  understanding of the problem was flawed, and it's
  not a widespread issue.
- **Your unique value proposition is not resonating or
  is easily copied and defensible:** You find that your
  differentiation isn't strong enough, or competitors

are easily replicating your offering, making it difficult to establish a sustainable competitive advantage. Your "why" might be strong, but your "what" or "how" isn't unique enough.

- **A major external shift makes your original idea irrelevant or unsustainable:** A new, disruptive technology emerges, significant regulatory changes occur, or market needs fundamentally shift in a way that renders your original idea obsolete or unviable. For example, a physical DVD rental service would have needed to pivot drastically with the rise of streaming.

- **You discover a more compelling problem or solution (the "discovery pivot"):** Through your iterative process and deep market engagement, you accidentally stumble upon an even greater opportunity, a more painful problem, or a fundamentally more effective way to solve a related problem that you hadn't initially considered. This is often the most exciting type of pivot, leading to unforeseen success.

The decision to pivot or persist is rarely easy, often fraught with emotional attachment to your original vision, and typically involves a complex mix of objective data analysis, informed intuition, and honest self-assessment. It requires immense courage to let go of what isn't working, even if you've invested heavily, and profound humility to admit when your initial assumptions were wrong. However, making the right decision at the right time is absolutely crucial for long-term growth and avoiding the sunk cost fallacy. Don't be afraid to pivot; it's not a sign of failure but a hallmark of intelligence, adaptability, and strategic foresight. Many of the most successful companies in history (e.g., YouTube started as a dating site, Slack as a gaming company) started with a completely different idea, demonstrating that the ability to pivot is often more valuable than the initial idea itself.

Overcoming obstacles is not about avoiding them, as they are an inevitable part of any worthwhile journey. Instead, it's about developing the mental fortitude, the creative problem-solving skills, and the strategic wisdom to navigate them effectively. By anticipating challenges proactively, fostering a culture of creative solution-finding, and knowing when to pivot or persist based on clear data and a strong "why," you transform roadblocks into powerful stepping stones. This ensures your ideas continue to grow, evolve, and ultimately reach their fullest potential, making a real impact in the world. In the next part of the book, we will shift our focus to taking decisive action and building unstoppable momentum, leveraging the robust mindset and refined ideas you've cultivated.

Part 3

Bringing Your Ideas to Life

(Action & Impact)

Chapter 9

Taking Decisive Action: The Momentum Multiplier

You've diligently done the foundational work. You've cultivated a resilient, optimistic, and curious mindset, equipped with self-compassion to navigate the inevitable bumps in the road (Part 1). You've learned to generate compelling ideas, shape a clear and inspiring vision, engage in the crucial process of prototyping and testing, and even anticipate and strategically navigate obstacles (Part 2). All of this intellectual preparation, emotional cultivation, and strategic planning is not merely vital; it is absolutely indispensable for setting the stage. However, all this preparation leads to this singular, crucial point: **action.** An idea, no matter how brilliant its conception, how meticulously planned its execution, or how deeply it resonates with your "why," remains a mere thought, a potentiality, until it is brought to life through decisive, consistent, and deliberate effort. This chapter marks the powerful beginning of **Part 3: Bringing Your Ideas to Life (Action & Impact)**, focusing intensely on how to transform your refined vision into a tangible, impactful reality by becoming a true master of execution.

Thinking deeply about your idea is important. Planning strategically for your idea is essential. But **doing** – taking consistent, concrete steps – is the ultimate momentum multiplier. It's the irresistible force that propels your idea forward, gathers invaluable real-world feedback, reveals new insights that theory alone cannot provide, and ultimately creates the desired impact you envision. Without decisive action, even the most meticulously planned, brilliantly conceived, and passionately held ideas will languish in the realm of potential, never seeing the light of day. They become forgotten dreams, victims of inertia. This chapter will equip you with a powerful arsenal of strategies designed to break through any lingering inertia, build powerful and sustainable habits, and conquer the pervasive and often debilitating challenge of procrastination that can derail even the most promising ventures.

Breaking Down Big Goals

One of the most common and paralyzing reasons ideas stall, even after extensive planning, is that the sheer perceived scale of the ultimate vision feels utterly overwhelming. A grand, audacious goal, like "launch a successful global tech startup" or "write a bestselling, critically acclaimed novel," can feel like an insurmountable mountain range, a distant peak shrouded in mist. Our brains, when confronted with such a massive, undefined undertaking, often default to self-protective mechanisms like procrastination or complete paralysis. The path seems too long, too complex, and the first step too ambiguous. The key, the absolute secret, to initiating and sustaining consistent action is to **systematically break down these big, ambitious, and often intimidating goals into smaller, more manageable, and immediately actionable steps.**

Think of it like the classic adage: "How do you eat an elephant? One bite at a time." Each "bite" is a small, concrete, and clearly defined task that you can realistically complete within a reasonable timeframe, often within a single day, or even just a few focused hours. This granular approach offers several powerful and interconnected benefits that directly combat overwhelm and foster progress:

1. **Reduces Overwhelm and Cognitive Load:** Faced with a single, massive goal, your brain sees an undifferentiated blob of complexity. This triggers a stress response, making it hard to even know where to begin. Conversely, a clearly defined list of 50 or 100 small, distinct tasks feels significantly less daunting. Each small task is a clear, unambiguous instruction for your brain, making it far easier to initiate action. It transforms a mountain into a series of manageable hills.

2. **Builds Irreversible Momentum:** Completing a small task, even a tiny one, provides an immediate and

tangible sense of accomplishment. This "mini-win" is not just a psychological boost; it triggers the release of dopamine in your brain, a powerful neurotransmitter associated with reward, motivation, and learning. This creates a positive feedback loop: you complete a task, feel good, and are then more motivated to take the next step. This compounding momentum is crucial for sustaining long-term effort and preventing burnout.

3. **Provides Unprecedented Clarity and Foresight:** The very act of breaking down a large goal forces you to think through the actual, granular steps required to achieve it. This process often reveals potential roadblocks, necessary resources, or dependencies you might not have considered when viewing the goal as a single entity. It transforms abstract notions into concrete plans, allowing you to anticipate challenges (as discussed in Chapter 8) and plan for them more effectively.

4. **Enables Transparent Tracking and Celebration of Progress:** It's incredibly difficult to gauge progress on a vague, monolithic goal. However, when you're checking off small, completed tasks regularly, it's easy to see and celebrate your advancement. This visual representation of continuous forward movement is a powerful motivator, especially during challenging periods. It provides tangible proof that

you are indeed moving closer to your vision, reinforcing your belief in your capabilities.

5. **Facilitates Agile Iteration and Adaptation:** Smaller, modular steps allow for quicker feedback and easier adjustments. If a small piece of your plan isn't working as expected, or if new information comes to light (as in the prototyping and testing phase), it's far simpler and less costly to pivot, refine, or even discard that small piece than to overhaul a massive, undifferentiated project. This agility is critical in today's rapidly changing environment, allowing your idea to evolve responsively.

How to break down your goals effectively:

- **Start with your Strategic Goal:** Begin with one of your mid-term strategic goals (e.g., "Launch beta version of the app by Q4," or "Secure initial seed funding," or "Complete the first draft of my book manuscript"). This is your immediate focus.

- **Deconstruct into Tactical Goals (Major Milestones):** What are the 3-5 major components or milestones needed to achieve that strategic goal? (e.g., for the app launch: "Develop core features," "Design user interface," "Set up user testing," "Prepare marketing materials," "Deploy to app stores"). These are the larger chunks of work.

- **Break into Specific, Actionable Tasks (Micro-Steps):** For each tactical goal, list the individual, concrete, and unambiguous actions required. Make them verbs, and ensure they are small enough to be completed in a single focused session.

    - *For "Develop core features":* "Write user stories for feature X," "Set up development environment," "Code login module," "Test login module."
    - *For "Design user interface":* "Research 5 competitor UI designs," "Sketch 5 UI layouts for screen Y," "Create high-fidelity mockups for screen Z," "Get feedback on mockups from 3 users."
    - *For "Prepare marketing materials":* "Draft social media launch posts," "Select target keywords for app store optimization," "Design app icon," "Write app store description."

- **Estimate Time and Prioritize:** Assign a rough, realistic time estimate to each task (e.g., 30 minutes, 2 hours, half a day). Then, prioritize them based on dependencies (what needs to be done before something else?) and impact (what will yield the most learning, progress, or value?). Use a simple A, B, C priority system or numerical ranking.

Tools like project management software (Trello, Asana, Monday.com, ClickUp), simple digital to-do lists (Todoist, Microsoft To Do), or even a physical notebook and pen can be invaluable for this process. The absolute key is to make your *next action* so small, so clear, and so immediately actionable that it feels almost impossible *not* to do it. This is the concept of a "minimum viable action" – the smallest possible step that moves you forward.

Building Consistent Habits

Decisive action isn't about relying on heroic bursts of effort, sporadic all-nighters, or waiting for a surge of motivation. While those moments can be exciting, they are unsustainable. True, long-term progress and the successful growth of your ideas come from the cumulative power of **consistent habits**. Your ideas will grow not through occasional grand gestures, but through the steady, relentless application of small, daily efforts. Habits are the invisible architects of your success; they are the automated behaviors that, over time, compound into massive results. They reduce the need for constant willpower, automate productive behaviors, and ensure continuous progress, even on days when motivation is low, energy is flagging, or distractions abound.

Think of an athlete training for a marathon, or a musician mastering an instrument. They don't achieve their goals through one massive, overwhelming session. Instead, they run a few miles consistently, practice a few scales daily, building up their endurance, skill, and muscle memory over time. Similarly, growing your idea requires consistent, disciplined "training" – small, repeated actions that build over days, weeks, months, and years.

Strategies for building powerful, idea-growing habits:

1. **Start Small, Make it Easy, and Focus on Identity:** The biggest mistake people make when trying to build new habits is trying to do too much too soon. If you want to write a book, don't aim for an hour a day initially; aim for just 15 minutes, or even just writing one single sentence. If you want to learn to code, start with 10 minutes of a tutorial or solving one simple problem. The goal in the beginning is not the output, but the *repetition* and the *identity*. You're not just doing a task; you're becoming "a writer," "a coder," "an innovator." Make the habit so easy, so trivial, that you literally cannot say no to doing it. Consistency in tiny acts trumps sporadic heroic efforts.

2. **Habit Stacking (Leverage Existing Routines):** Link a new desired habit to an existing, well-established habit that you already perform automatically. This leverages existing neural pathways and makes the new habit feel less like an effort.

The formula is: "After [CURRENT HABIT], I will [NEW HABIT]."

- "After I pour my morning coffee, I will spend 15 minutes outlining the next section of my idea."
- "After I finish dinner, I will review my project tasks for 10 minutes and plan my next day's actions."
- "After I brush my teeth at night, I will write down three ideas for my project in my idea journal."

3. **Design Your Environment for Success (and Failure Prevention):** Make it incredibly easy to do the right thing and significantly harder to do the wrong thing. This is about engineering your surroundings to support your goals.

- If you want to write, open your writing software and close all other distracting tabs *before* you go to bed, so it's ready when you wake up.
- If you want to work on your idea first thing in the morning, put your phone in another room or on airplane mode.
- If you're prone to social media distractions, use website blockers during your focused work times.
- Keep your workspace tidy and organized to reduce mental clutter. Remove temptations.

4. **Track Your Progress Visually (The "Don't Break the Chain" Method):** Use a habit tracker app, a simple calendar where you mark an "X" for each day you perform your habit, or a dedicated journal. Seeing your streak grow is incredibly motivating and creates a powerful visual positive feedback loop. It taps into our desire for consistency and our aversion to breaking a visible chain of progress. This visual reinforcement helps cement the habit.

5. **Don't Break the Chain (But Forgive Yourself If You Do):** The ultimate goal is consistency, not perfection. The aim is to build a long, unbroken chain of successful habit repetitions. However, life happens. If you miss a day, don't despair, don't beat yourself up, and don't let one lapse derail your entire effort. Practice self-compassion (Chapter 4!). Acknowledge the miss, forgive yourself immediately, and then commit to getting back on track the very next day. The rule is: "Never miss twice." One missed day is an anomaly; two missed days start a new, negative pattern.

6. **Reward Yourself (Appropriately and Intelligently):** After consistently performing a habit for a period (e.g., a week, a month), give yourself a small, non-detrimental reward. This reinforces the positive association with the habit. The reward should be something you genuinely enjoy but that doesn't

undermine the habit itself. For example, after a week of consistent writing, you might allow yourself to watch an episode of your favorite show, buy a new book, or enjoy a special coffee. The reward should be immediate enough to link to the habit, but not so immediate that it becomes a distraction.

Consistent habits create compounding returns, much like compound interest in finance. Small, consistent actions over time lead to massive, often exponential, results that are far beyond what sporadic bursts of effort can ever achieve. It's the daily grind, the quiet persistence, that builds empires of ideas.

Overcoming Procrastination

Procrastination is the silent thief of dreams, the insidious enemy of action. It's not merely laziness; it's the frustrating and often self-defeating gap between knowing what you *should* do and actually *doing* it. It's a complex psychological phenomenon, often a symptom of deeper issues: a fear of failure (or even success), feeling overwhelmed by the task's magnitude, perfectionism (as discussed earlier), a lack of clarity on the next step, or simply the perceived unpleasantness of the task itself. Understanding its root cause – whether it's anxiety, boredom, or a lack of self-regulation – is the crucial first step to effectively overcoming it.

Strategies to conquer procrastination and reclaim your productive flow:

1. **The 2-Minute Rule (and its Extension):** If a task takes less than two minutes to complete, do it immediately. This simple rule, popularized by David Allen, builds immediate momentum and clears small, nagging items from your mental to-do list, reducing cognitive load. Examples: sending a quick email, making a phone call, tidying your workspace, replying to a message, putting away dishes. The extension: If a task takes more than two minutes, but you can *start* it in two minutes, then just start it. Often, once you begin, the inertia breaks, and you find yourself continuing.

2. **The Pomodoro Technique (Focused Sprints):** This time management method, developed by Francesco Cirillo, involves working in focused, timed bursts. Set a timer for 25 minutes (one "Pomodoro"), dedicate yourself fully to one single task during that time, without any distractions, and then take a mandatory 5-minute break. After four "Pomodoros," take a longer break (15-30 minutes). This structured approach helps maintain intense focus, prevents burnout, and makes daunting tasks seem more manageable by breaking them into smaller, timed chunks. The ticking timer creates a gentle urgency that can override procrastination.

3. **Identify the "Next Action" (Clarity is King):** Often, procrastination stems not from laziness, but from a lack of clarity on what the very next, concrete step is. If you're stuck on a vague task like "Develop marketing strategy," break it down ruthlessly: "Research 3 competitor marketing campaigns," "Brainstorm 10 potential taglines," "Schedule a meeting with a marketing mentor." Focus only on that single, immediate, bite-sized next action. When you know exactly what to do, the mental barrier to starting significantly diminishes.

4. **Tackle the Hardest Task First (Eat the Frog):** Mark Twain famously said, "Eat a live frog first thing in the morning and nothing worse will happen to you the rest of the day." Identify your most daunting, unpleasant, or energy-draining task (your "frog") and tackle it first thing in your workday. Once it's done, the rest of your day feels significantly easier, you gain a powerful sense of accomplishment, and you build significant momentum that carries through your other tasks. This strategy leverages your peak willpower and energy levels.

5. **Accountability (External Motivation):** Tell someone about your goals and what specific tasks you intend to complete by a certain time. This could be a friend, a mentor, an accountability partner, or even a public commitment on social media. Knowing someone is

expecting an update or will check in on your progress can be a powerful external motivator that helps you overcome the internal resistance of procrastination. Regular check-ins can create a healthy pressure to perform.

6. **Remove Distractions and Optimize Your Environment:** Your environment plays a massive role in your ability to focus. Turn off all unnecessary notifications on your phone and computer. Close irrelevant browser tabs. Put your phone in another room or on airplane mode. Use noise-canceling headphones if needed. Create a physical and digital environment that is conducive to focused work and minimizes temptations. The less friction there is to starting, the easier it is to act.

7. **Forgive Yourself and Restart Immediately (Self-Compassion in Action):** If you do procrastinate, and you inevitably will, don't beat yourself up with harsh self-criticism. As discussed in Chapter 4, this only fuels the cycle of avoidance. Acknowledge the lapse without judgment, forgive yourself with compassion, and then immediately re-engage with the task. Don't let one lapse derail your entire effort or lead to a spiral of self-sabotage. The power is in your ability to restart, not in never stopping.

8. **Connect to Your "Why" (Purpose-Driven Motivation):** When motivation wanes and the urge to procrastinate becomes strong, revisit your deepest "why" (Chapter 6). Remind yourself of the profound impact you want to make, the problem you're passionate about solving, and the vision you're striving to achieve. This purpose-driven motivation can often override the immediate discomfort or perceived unpleasantness of the task, providing a powerful intrinsic reason to act. Visualizing the positive outcome can be a strong antidote to the short-term pain of effort.

Decisive action is the indispensable bridge between intention and tangible impact. By systematically breaking down overwhelming goals into manageable steps, building consistent and powerful habits that automate progress, and mastering a suite of strategies to overcome procrastination, you transform your ideas from mere concepts into living, breathing, and evolving realities. This unwavering commitment to consistent execution is what truly multiplies your momentum, ensures your ideas not only grow but thrive, and ultimately creates the meaningful change you envision in the world. In the next chapter, we will explore the critical importance of building and leveraging your support system – the people who will champion you and your ideas.

Chapter 10

Building Your Support System

You've diligently mastered the art of decisive action, breaking down formidable goals into manageable steps, cultivating consistent and powerful habits, and strategically conquering the insidious challenge of procrastination. You are now actively transforming your deeply refined ideas into tangible reality, building momentum with every deliberate step. Yet, even the most determined, resilient, and action-oriented individual cannot achieve true, sustained growth, profound impact, or lasting fulfillment in isolation. The journey of growing an idea, whether it's a deeply personal project, a groundbreaking artistic endeavor, or a world-changing entrepreneurial venture, is inherently complex, filled with moments of profound doubt, unexpected setbacks, intricate problems requiring specialized knowledge, and the constant need for fresh, diverse perspectives. This chapter emphasizes the absolutely critical importance of **building and strategically leveraging your support system** – not just a casual collection of acquaintances, but a carefully cultivated network of people who will champion your vision, challenge you constructively when needed, actively collaborate with you, and provide the essential emotional and practical scaffolding for your continued growth and the flourishing of your ideas.

Think of any great achievement in history, from the most monumental scientific breakthroughs to the most timeless artistic masterpieces or the most enduringly successful businesses. Behind every singular name that history remembers, there was invariably a dedicated team, a vibrant community, a supportive family, or a robust network of individuals who contributed their unique talents, offered unwavering support, provided crucial resources, and, most importantly, believed in the vision when others might have doubted. You are not an island, and attempting to grow your idea in solitude is not only incredibly inefficient and resource-intensive, but it is also profoundly unsustainable, leading quickly to burnout, limited perspective, and missed opportunities. The collective wisdom, diverse skills, and shared emotional burden of a strong support system are your secret weapons.

The Value of Mentors and Collaborators

As you navigate the intricate complexities of bringing your idea to life, from initial concept to full-scale implementation, you will inevitably encounter challenges that exceed your current knowledge, skills, or experience. This is not a sign of weakness, but a natural part of growth. This is precisely where the unparalleled value of **mentors and collaborators** becomes indispensable. They are not merely passive advisors or occasional sounding boards; they are active guides, co-creators, and powerful accelerants of your personal and professional growth, helping you to transcend your current limitations.

Mentors: A mentor is a seasoned individual with significantly more experience than you in a particular area, who is willing to generously share their wisdom, hard-won insights, and strategic guidance. A true mentor invests in your growth, offering not just advice, but a deeper understanding of the landscape. They can offer:

- **Experienced Perspective and Foresight:** Mentors have likely faced and overcome similar challenges to the ones you're currently grappling with, or will soon encounter. They can offer invaluable strategies, highlight potential pitfalls to avoid (saving you immense time and costly mistakes), and provide a broader, more nuanced view of the industry or domain landscape. They possess the unique ability to "see around corners," anticipating future trends or common stumbling blocks that a less experienced individual might miss entirely. This foresight is a priceless asset.

- **Accelerated Knowledge Transfer:** A mentor can teach you specific skills, decode complex industry nuances, explain unspoken best practices, or clarify intricate processes that would otherwise take you years of trial and error to learn on your own. They can distill years of experience into actionable lessons, effectively fast-tracking your learning curve. This direct transmission of practical knowledge is far more efficient than theoretical study alone.

- **Accountability and Encouragement (The Balanced Approach):** A good mentor provides a crucial sounding board for your ideas and concerns. They will hold you accountable to your goals, gently but firmly pushing you to meet commitments, while simultaneously offering genuine encouragement and emotional support during setbacks. They celebrate your wins and help you process your losses, ensuring you don't get stuck in self-pity but rather learn and move forward.

- **Network Access and Strategic Connections:** Mentors often have extensive professional networks built over years. They can introduce you to valuable contacts – potential investors, strategic partners, key customers, or other experts – opening doors to opportunities you might not otherwise access for years, if ever. A single introduction from a trusted mentor can unlock exponential growth.

- **Constructive, Unbiased Feedback:** Unlike friends or family who might be overly supportive (and thus, less helpful for critical evaluation), a mentor can provide honest, objective, and actionable feedback on your ideas, your approach, and even your personal development. Their perspective is often detached enough to see flaws or opportunities that you, being too close to the work, might miss. This kind of feedback, though sometimes difficult to hear, is essential for true refinement and growth.

How to find and effectively engage mentors:

- **Identify Your Specific Needs:** Before seeking a mentor, clarify what specific areas you need guidance in. Is it marketing strategy, fundraising, product development, team leadership, navigating career transitions, or something else entirely? The more specific you are, the better you can target your search.

- **Look in Unexpected Places:** Don't just target famous figures or industry titans. Often, the most effective mentors are individuals who are just a few steps ahead of you in your field, or even in related fields where their experience might be highly transferable. Look within your existing network, professional associations, alumni groups, or even online communities.

- **Offer Value First and Build a Relationship:** Approach potential mentors by showing genuine interest in *their* work, their journey, and their insights. Don't immediately ask for a huge time commitment. Start by offering something in return, even if it's just your enthusiasm, your willingness to help them in a small way, or simply a thoughtful question about their experience. Build a relationship organically before making a formal "ask."

- **Be Respectful of Their Time and Prepared:** When you do get their time, come prepared with specific, well-thought-out questions. Be concise in your explanations and follow up promptly with thanks and updates on how you've applied their advice. Demonstrate that their time and wisdom are valued.

- **Formal vs. Informal Mentorship:** Understand that mentorship can take many forms. It can be a formal, structured arrangement with regular meetings, or it can be an informal, organic relationship built over time through genuine connection, where you occasionally seek advice as needed. Both are valuable.

Collaborators: While mentors provide guidance and wisdom, collaborators actively work *with* you, shoulder-to-shoulder, to build, refine, and execute your idea. They bring complementary skills, diverse perspectives, and crucially, shared ownership and responsibility to the venture.

- **Complementary Skills and Expertise:** You cannot be an expert in everything, nor should you try to be. Collaborators fill critical skill gaps (e.g., a visionary founder partnering with a technical expert, a creative designer teaming up with a business strategist). This division of labor allows each person to focus on their strengths, leading to higher quality work and faster progress.

- **Diverse Perspectives and Creative Synergy:** Different backgrounds, life experiences, and thinking styles lead to more robust ideas, more comprehensive problem-solving, and richer solutions. Collaborators challenge your assumptions, broaden your creative scope, and often see possibilities or risks that you, operating in your own echo chamber, might miss. The synergy of working together often leads to breakthroughs that wouldn't be possible individually.

- **Shared Workload and Mutual Accountability:** Growing an idea, especially a significant one, can be an immense amount of work. Collaborators share the burden, accelerate progress, and provide crucial mutual accountability. Knowing someone else is relying on you, and that you're relying on them, creates a powerful incentive to perform and stay committed.

- **Emotional Support and Resilience:** The journey of innovation is a rollercoaster. Sharing the highs of success and the lows of setbacks with someone who is equally invested can significantly reduce feelings of isolation, loneliness, and burnout. Having a partner to celebrate with and commiserate with strengthens your emotional resilience.

- **Increased Innovation and Problem Solving:** When multiple minds are focused on a problem, the potential for innovative solutions multiplies. Brainstorming sessions are richer, problem-solving discussions are more thorough, and the collective intelligence often leads to more elegant and effective outcomes.

How to find and effectively engage collaborators:

- **Clearly Define Roles, Expectations, and Agreements:** Before partnering, ensure everyone involved has an absolutely clear understanding of their responsibilities, decision-making authority, equity splits (if applicable), and how conflicts will be resolved. A clear, written agreement (even a simple one initially) can prevent major misunderstandings down the line.

- **Look for Shared Vision, Values, and Complementary Strengths:** Beyond just skills, ensure potential collaborators deeply align with your "why" (Chapter 6) and core values. Misaligned values can lead to significant friction, even if skills are perfectly matched. Seek individuals whose strengths complement your weaknesses, creating a well-rounded team.

- **Start Small and Test the Waters:** Before committing to a long-term, high-stakes partnership, test the waters with a small, low-risk project or a limited engagement. This allows you to assess working styles, communication patterns, and commitment levels without significant upfront investment.

- **Communicate Openly, Honestly, and Continuously:** Regular, transparent, and empathetic communication is the bedrock of successful collaboration. Establish clear channels and rhythms for communication. Be honest about challenges, progress, and feelings. Address conflicts directly and constructively, focusing on the problem, not the person.

Surrounding Yourself with Growth-Minded Individuals

Your immediate environment, both physical and social, profoundly impacts your mindset and, by extension, your ability to grow your ideas. Just as deeply ingrained limiting beliefs can hold you back, surrounding yourself with individuals who embody a fixed mindset – those who are cynical, resistant to change, constantly focus on problems rather than solutions, or are quick to dismiss new ideas – can subtly but powerfully erode your optimism, resilience, and creative drive. Their negativity can be contagious, pulling you down. Conversely, deliberately immersing yourself in a community of **growth-minded individuals** acts as an incredibly powerful accelerant for your personal and professional development.

Growth-minded individuals are those who:

- **Embrace Learning and Challenges with Enthusiasm:** They see setbacks not as failures, but as invaluable opportunities for learning and personal development. They are eager to acquire new knowledge and skills, viewing challenges as puzzles to be solved.

- **Are Inherently Curious and Open to New Ideas:** They are receptive to different perspectives, willing to experiment, and eager to explore uncharted territory. They ask "why not?" rather than "why?"

- **Celebrate Others' Successes Genuinely:** They are not threatened by the achievements of others; instead, they are genuinely happy for your progress and offer sincere encouragement and support. They see success as abundant, not a zero-sum game.

- **Provide Constructive, Actionable Criticism:** They offer feedback that is honest, specific, and delivered with the sole intent to help you improve. Their criticism is never personal or destructive; it's always aimed at growth.

- **Are Proactive and Action-Oriented:** They don't just talk about ideas or complain about problems; they actively work to bring solutions to fruition. They are doers, not just dreamers.

- **Maintain a Positive Outlook:** While realistic, they maintain an underlying optimism, believing in the possibility of positive outcomes and solutions, even in difficult circumstances.

How to cultivate a growth-minded circle around you:

1. **Actively Join Relevant Communities and Networks:** Seek out professional associations, industry-specific groups, online forums, specialized mastermind groups, or local meetups related to your interests or your idea. These are natural breeding grounds for like-minded individuals who share your aspirations and challenges. Participate actively, ask questions, and offer your own insights.

2. **Attend Workshops, Conferences, and Seminars with Intent:** These events are not just for learning content; they are prime opportunities to connect with people who share your aspirations, are engaged in similar work, and face similar challenges. Go with the intention of networking and building genuine connections, not just collecting business cards. Follow up thoughtfully with people you connect with.

3. **Be Intentional in Curating Your Relationships:** Consciously evaluate the impact of the people in your life. Seek to spend more time with individuals who uplift, inspire, challenge you positively, and energize you. Conversely, limit your exposure to those who consistently drain your energy, foster negativity, or discourage your efforts. This isn't about cutting off old friends, but about consciously curating your inner circle to ensure it actively supports your growth journey.

4. **Be a Growth-Minded Individual Yourself:** The most effective way to attract growth-minded people into your orbit is to embody those very qualities yourself. Be curious, supportive, open to feedback, willing to share your own learnings and struggles, and genuinely interested in the growth of others. Your positive energy and proactive approach will naturally attract similar individuals.

5. **Create Your Own Mastermind or Accountability Group:** If you can't find the perfect existing group, create one! Invite a few individuals who inspire you, whose work you admire, and who you believe would benefit from a structured support system. Agree to meet regularly (e.g., weekly or bi-weekly) to discuss ideas, share progress, offer constructive feedback, and provide mutual accountability and support. These small, dedicated groups can become incredibly powerful engines of collective growth.

This isn't about abandoning your existing social circle, but about consciously and strategically curating your inner circle to ensure it actively supports and amplifies your growth journey. The collective energy, shared wisdom, diverse perspectives, and mutual encouragement within a growth-minded community can be an unparalleled source of strength, inspiration, and resilience.

Effective Communication

Building and maintaining a robust support system, whether it involves formal mentors, dedicated collaborators, or your wider community of growth-minded individuals, hinges entirely on the bedrock of **effective communication**. Your ability to articulate your vision with clarity, convey your needs precisely, listen actively and empathetically, and manage expectations transparently is paramount. Miscommunication is a silent killer of relationships and projects; it can lead to misunderstandings, missed opportunities, fractured partnerships, and eroded trust, thereby undermining the very support you're trying to build.

Key aspects of effective communication for nurturing your support system:

1. **Clarity and Conciseness:** When explaining your idea, asking for help, or providing updates, be clear, direct, and concise. Respect others' valuable time by getting straight to the point, avoiding jargon where possible, and structuring your message logically. Use the clarity of your "why" and goals (Chapter 6) to guide your message, ensuring it resonates with your audience. Avoid rambling or burying the lead.

2. **Active Listening:** Just as important, if not more so, than speaking is listening. Practice active listening by giving your full, undivided attention when others

are speaking. Avoid interrupting. Ask clarifying questions to ensure you've understood their message correctly ("So, what I hear you saying is..."). Reflect back what you've heard in your own words to confirm understanding. This builds profound trust, shows respect, and prevents misunderstandings from festering.

3. **Empathy and Understanding:** Strive to understand the other person's perspective, their motivations, their constraints, and their emotional state. This is particularly important when receiving feedback, navigating disagreements, or discussing sensitive topics. Put yourself in their shoes. Acknowledge their feelings ("I understand this might be frustrating for you"). Empathy fosters stronger bonds and more productive interactions.

4. **Setting Clear Expectations:** Be explicit and transparent about what you need from others, what you can offer in return, and what the scope of the interaction or collaboration is. For example: "I need 30 minutes of your time for advice on X, and I'll send you specific questions beforehand." "I'm looking for a collaborator to handle the technical development, with a clear equity split and defined responsibilities." "I need honest, critical feedback on this prototype, not just praise." Unstated expectations are a common source of conflict and disappointment.

5. **Providing and Receiving Feedback Constructively:** Feedback is the lifeblood of growth. When *giving* feedback, focus on the idea, the behavior, or the process, not the person ("This approach could be refined" instead of "You made a mistake"). Be specific, provide examples, and offer solutions or suggestions for improvement. When *receiving* feedback, practice the non-defensiveness and curiosity discussed in Chapter 7. See it as a valuable gift for improvement, even if it stings initially. Ask clarifying questions and thank the person for their honesty.

6. **Regular and Thoughtful Updates:** Keep your support system informed of your progress, challenges, and successes. This keeps them engaged, invested in your journey, and allows them to offer timely support or celebrate your milestones. Don't just reach out when you need something. Share your learnings, your small wins, and your pivots. This consistent communication fosters a sense of partnership and shared purpose.

7. **Conflict Resolution:** In any close working relationship, disagreements will arise. Approach conflicts as opportunities for deeper understanding and stronger solutions, rather than as personal attacks. Focus on the issue, not the individual. Seek win-win solutions. Be willing to compromise and, if necessary, agree to disagree respectfully. The ability to navigate conflict constructively is a hallmark of mature, effective teams.

Building a robust, dynamic support system is not a luxury; it's a strategic imperative and a fundamental component of sustainable growth for both your ideas and your mindset. By actively seeking out and nurturing relationships with mentors and collaborators, intentionally surrounding yourself with growth-minded individuals, and consistently practicing effective, empathetic communication, you create an invaluable ecosystem of support. This network will amplify your efforts, accelerate your learning, provide crucial emotional resilience, and sustain you through every challenging yet rewarding phase of your journey. You don't have to do it alone, and indeed, you shouldn't. The collective strength of your support system will be one of your greatest assets. In the next chapter, we will discuss the vital practice of measuring progress and sustaining growth, ensuring your efforts lead to lasting impact.

Chapter 11

Measuring Progress and Sustaining Growth

You've embarked on an incredible, transformative journey. You've diligently cultivated a resilient, optimistic, and curious mindset, fortified by self-compassion (Part 1). You've learned to generate powerful, impactful ideas, shape them with a clear vision, engage in the crucial process of iterative prototyping and testing, strategically overcome inevitable obstacles, take decisive and consistent action, and wisely build a robust support system (Part 2 and earlier chapters in Part 3). Your idea is no longer just a fleeting concept or a theoretical blueprint; it's a living, breathing entity, gaining tangible momentum, attracting engagement, and starting to create the impact you envisioned. But here's a fundamental truth often overlooked: the journey doesn't culminate with a single launch, a major milestone, or even initial success. True, sustainable growth, both for your cherished idea and for yourself as its creator and champion, is an ongoing, continuous process – a marathon, not a sprint. This chapter focuses intently on the vital, interconnected practices of **measuring progress and sustaining growth**, ensuring that your dedicated efforts lead to lasting, meaningful impact and that you, along with your ideas, continue to evolve, adapt, and flourish in an ever-changing world.

Without clear, objective ways to measure your progress, you're essentially flying blind, unable to discern what's working, what isn't, or whether you're even moving in the right direction. Without a deliberate strategy for sustenance and continuous improvement, even the most brilliant and initially successful ideas can eventually stagnate, become irrelevant, or be surpassed by more agile competitors. This crucial phase is about establishing intelligent feedback loops, celebrating achievements strategically to fuel motivation, and cultivating the unwavering discipline to continuously learn, adapt, and improve. It's about building a perpetual motion machine for growth.

Defining Success on Your Terms

In a world relentlessly obsessed with external, often superficial, metrics – revenue figures, social media likes, viral reach, public recognition, competitor comparisons – it's incredibly easy to lose sight of what truly, deeply matters to *you* and your unique "why." While external validation can certainly be motivating and provide useful market signals, allowing it to be your sole arbiter of success is a dangerous trap. It can lead to burnout, misalignment with your core purpose, and a profound sense of emptiness even in the face of apparent achievement. Therefore, it is absolutely crucial to **define success on your own terms**, aligning it intrinsically with your core "why" (as articulated with such clarity in Chapter 6) and your deepest personal values. If your idea is primarily a passion project, success might be measured in terms of creative fulfillment, the joy of the process, or the positive impact on a small, dedicated community, rather than purely financial gain. If it's a business venture, financial viability is undoubtedly key, but perhaps it's balanced with equally important metrics like ethical practices, employee well-being, environmental sustainability, or the depth of customer relationships.

Defining success on your terms involves a profound act of introspection and conscious choice:

1. **Revisiting Your "Why" as the Ultimate Compass:** Your "why" is not just a motivational statement; it is the ultimate, non-negotiable measure of your idea's true success. Periodically ask yourself: Is your idea consistently fulfilling its core purpose? Is it actively creating the specific change you genuinely want to see in the world? Is it solving the problem it set out to solve in a meaningful way? Use this "why" as your primary filter for evaluating progress. For example, if your "why" is "to empower underserved communities through accessible education," then simply having a large number of users isn't enough if those users aren't from the target community, or if the education isn't truly empowering.

2. **Aligning with Personal Values for Sustainable Fulfillment:** Does the pursuit, development, and growth of this idea align authentically with your personal values for work-life balance, integrity, transparency, continuous learning, creative expression, or contribution to society? Success that compromises your deeply held values often feels hollow, unsustainable, and can lead to moral fatigue or resentment, even if it brings external accolades. For instance, achieving high revenue might be a metric, but if it required unethical marketing tactics that violate your integrity, is it truly success on *your* terms?

3. **Looking Beyond Solely Tangible Metrics (The Qualitative Dimension):** While quantifiable metrics are undeniably important for tracking progress, don't let them be your *only* definition of success. Consider the equally vital qualitative aspects that contribute to a rich and meaningful journey:
   - **Personal Growth:** How have *you* grown as an individual throughout this challenging yet rewarding journey? What new skills have you acquired (e.g., public speaking, coding, negotiation, empathy)? What limiting beliefs (from Chapter 1) have you actively overcome? What new strengths have you discovered within yourself? Documenting these personal transformations is a powerful form of success.

- **Impact Stories and Testimonials:** What real-world, tangible difference is your idea making for your target audience or community? Are you genuinely solving their problem effectively? Collect specific stories, testimonials, and qualitative feedback that illustrate the human impact of your work. For a mental wellness app, success might be measured by user testimonials about reduced anxiety, not just download numbers.

  - **Fulfillment and Meaning:** Does working on this idea consistently bring you joy, a deep sense of meaning, and purpose? Are you engaged and energized by the process, even amidst challenges? This intrinsic satisfaction is a powerful indicator of sustainable success.

  - **Learning and Insight:** What new insights have you gained about your problem, your audience, your industry, or even yourself? How has your understanding of the problem or solution deepened through the iterative process? The acquisition of knowledge and wisdom is a profound form of success.

4. **Setting Internal Benchmarks and Celebrating Personal Progress:** Instead of constantly comparing yourself, your idea, or your progress to others (which can be a demotivating trap, especially with the curated realities presented on social media), set

benchmarks based on your own unique progress and potential. Are you doing better than you were last month, last quarter, or last year? Are you consistently improving on your own best efforts? This fosters a healthier, more sustainable sense of achievement and self-efficacy, focusing on your unique trajectory rather than an external, often unattainable, ideal. Your journey is unique, and so should be your primary measure of success.

Defining success on your terms provides a clear, unwavering internal compass that prevents you from chasing external validation at the expense of your true purpose, your values, and your well-being. It empowers you to celebrate achievements that genuinely matter to you, fostering a deeper, more authentic sense of accomplishment.

Tracking Your Journey (Metrics and Milestones)

While your ultimate definition of success is deeply personal and qualitative, tracking your journey with objective **metrics and milestones** is absolutely essential for understanding concrete progress, making informed, data-driven decisions, and maintaining critical momentum. This is precisely where the "measurable" aspect of your SMART goals (from Chapter 6) comes powerfully into play. The adage "What gets measured gets managed, and what gets managed can be improved" holds profound truth. Without systematic tracking, your efforts risk becoming unfocused, and your ability to course-correct is severely limited.

Key Principles for Effective Tracking:

1. **Focus on Both Leading and Lagging Indicators (The Predictive Power):**
    - **Lagging Indicators:** These measure past performance or outcomes. They tell you what *has happened*. Examples include total sales figures, total number of users, project completion rates, profit margins, or the number of books sold. While crucial for understanding results, they are historical and don't tell you *why* something happened or what to do next.
    - **Leading Indicators:** These measure activities that predict future performance or outcomes. They tell you what *is happening now* and allow you to make proactive adjustments before it's too late. Examples include the number of user interviews conducted, the number of marketing campaigns launched, the number of prototypes built and tested, hours spent coding new features, or the number of networking meetings attended. Focus heavily on leading indicators, as they are within your direct control and directly influence the lagging indicators you ultimately care about. For a

non-profit, a lagging indicator might be "total donations received," while a leading indicator is "number of outreach events held." For a personal blog, "total page views" is lagging, but "number of posts published per week" is leading.

2. **Choose Relevant Metrics (Key Performance Indicators - KPIs):** Resist the temptation to track everything. Data overload leads to paralysis. Instead, identify the 3-5 most important metrics (Key Performance Indicators, or KPIs) that directly reflect the health and progress of your idea and, crucially, align with your "why." These are the vital signs of your project.
   - *For a digital product (e.g., an app):* User engagement (e.g., daily active users, average session time, feature usage), conversion rates (e.g., free-to-paid conversion), customer retention (e.g., churn rate), customer satisfaction (e.g., Net Promoter Score - NPS).
   - *For a service-based business:* Client acquisition rate, client satisfaction scores, referral rate, service delivery efficiency (e.g., time to complete a project), client lifetime value.
   - *For a creative project (e.g., writing a book):* Completion rate of chapters/sections, words written per day, audience engagement (e.g., reads, shares, comments on early drafts), feedback received on specific sections.

- *For personal growth (e.g., a new habit):* Consistency of the new habit (e.g., days exercised per week), number of new connections made, hours spent learning a new skill.

   Avoid "vanity metrics" – numbers that look good but don't actually reflect core progress or value (e.g., total website visitors if they don't convert).

3. **Establish Clear Baselines and Ambitious Targets:** Before you start measuring, know where you're starting from (your baseline) and where you want to go (your target). This provides essential context for your measurements and allows you to gauge actual progress. For example, if your baseline is 50 active users, a target of 500 users in three months provides a clear goal.

4. **Implement Regular Review Cadences:** Data is useless if it's not reviewed and analyzed. Schedule dedicated, non-negotiable time (e.g., weekly, bi-weekly, monthly, quarterly) to review your metrics. This isn't just about collecting data; it's about interpreting it. What do the numbers tell you? Are you on track to hit your goals? Are there any surprises or anomalies? What trends are emerging? What questions do the data raise? This review process is where insights are generated.

5. **Visualize Your Data for Clarity and Motivation:** Raw numbers can be overwhelming. Use charts, graphs, or simple dashboards to visualize your progress over time. Seeing trends, upward trajectories, or even dips can be incredibly insightful and motivating. Tools range from simple spreadsheets with built-in charting functions to dedicated analytics dashboards (e.g., Google Analytics, custom-built dashboards). Visual data makes it easier to spot patterns, communicate progress to your support system, and stay inspired.

6. **Strategically Celebrate Milestones:** As you hit your predefined milestones (from Chapter 6's goal breakdown and Chapter 9's task breakdown), take time to genuinely celebrate them. These are not just checkpoints; they are crucial opportunities to acknowledge effort, reinforce positive behavior, re-energize yourself and your team, and build collective morale. Celebrations don't have to be grand; they can be a team lunch, a personal treat, or simply a moment of quiet reflection and gratitude for the progress made. These moments are vital for sustaining long-term motivation and preventing burnout.

Effective tracking provides unparalleled clarity, highlights specific areas for improvement, and keeps you accountable to your vision and your "why." It transforms abstract effort into tangible progress.

Continuous Improvement (Feedback Loops, Adaptation, Avoiding Complacency)

The journey of growth, whether personal or for an idea, never truly ends. It's a dynamic, ongoing process. Even when your idea achieves significant success, the world continues to evolve at an accelerating pace, and so, too, must your approach. **Continuous improvement** is not merely a practice; it's a fundamental mindset – the relentless pursuit of seeking ways to enhance your idea, refine your processes, elevate your own capabilities, and deepen your impact. It's about establishing robust, multi-directional feedback loops, embracing perpetual adaptation as a core operating principle, and actively, vigilantly avoiding the insidious complacency that can lead to stagnation, decline, and ultimately, irrelevance.

1. **Formalize Robust Feedback Loops (Beyond Initial Testing):** While Chapter 7 focused on initial prototyping feedback, continuous improvement requires ongoing mechanisms for gathering insights from all angles.
   - **User/Customer Feedback:** Implement regular surveys (e.g., post-purchase, after a specific interaction), integrate feedback forms directly into your product/service, establish dedicated support channels (email, chat, phone), and actively engage in informal conversations or user forums. Actively solicit both positive

feedback (to understand what to double down on) and constructive criticism (to identify areas for improvement).

- **Team/Collaborator Feedback (Retrospectives):** If you're working with a team or collaborators, establish regular "retrospective" meetings. This is a dedicated time to discuss what's working well, what's not, what challenges were faced, and how processes can be improved for the next iteration. Foster a blame-free environment where honesty and learning are prioritized.
- **Self-Reflection (The Inner Feedback Loop):** Dedicate consistent time for personal reflection on your own performance, your learning journey, your emotional state, and your alignment with your "why." Journaling, meditation, or simply quiet contemplation can provide invaluable insights into your own patterns, strengths, and areas for personal growth. Are you still energized? Are you learning? Are you making the right decisions?

2. **Embrace Perpetual Adaptation (The Fluidity of Growth):** The world is fundamentally fluid and unpredictable. Technologies emerge and disrupt, markets shift rapidly, consumer behaviors evolve, and user needs are never static. Your idea, therefore, must be a living, breathing entity, inherently capable

of adapting and evolving. This means:

- **Staying Relentlessly Current:** Continuously fuel your curiosity and commit to lifelong learning (as discussed in Chapter 3). Read industry reports, follow thought leaders, attend webinars, and engage with emerging research to stay abreast of trends, new knowledge, and potential disruptions. Proactive learning allows you to anticipate, rather than just react.
- **Being Inherently Flexible:** Be willing to adjust your strategy, pivot your features, or even fundamentally refine your core offering in response to new information, validated feedback, or changing market conditions. Don't fall in love with your initial solution; fall in love with the *problem* you're solving. This detachment allows for necessary, sometimes painful, changes that ensure long-term viability.
- **Continuous Experimentation:** The small experiments you learned about in Chapter 7 are not just for the early stages. Continue running small, low-risk experiments to test new features, explore alternative marketing messages, optimize operational efficiencies, or explore new market segments.

This keeps your idea fresh, relevant, and continuously optimized.

3. **Actively Avoid Complacency (The Success Trap):** Success, paradoxically, can be one of the most dangerous traps for growth. When things are going well, there's a natural, human tendency to relax, to assume that what worked yesterday will continue to work tomorrow, and to stop innovating. This is the breeding ground for stagnation, allowing competitors to catch up and eventually surpass you. Complacency is the enemy of continuous improvement.

    o **Maintain a "Beginner's Mind" (Revisited):** Continuously approach your idea, your processes, and your industry with the curiosity, openness, and humility of a novice, even as you become an acknowledged expert. Always ask "why?" and "what if?"

    o **Set New, Ambitious Challenges:** Once a significant goal is achieved, resist the urge to rest on your laurels. Immediately set new, ambitious goals that push you and your idea further, forcing continued innovation and effort. This creates a continuous growth trajectory.

    o **Seek Disruption (Internally and Externally):** Periodically challenge your own assumptions, processes, and even your core business model. Engage in "red teaming" exercises, where you

imagine how a competitor might disrupt you, or how your own idea could be made obsolete. Actively seek out critical perspectives from those who might disagree with your current approach.

- ○ **Learn Deeply from Failures (Yours and Others'):** Don't just celebrate wins. Rigorously analyze failures (your own and those of others) to extract every possible lesson. What went wrong? Why? What could be done differently? This proactive learning from setbacks is a powerful defense against repeating mistakes and a catalyst for future success.

Measuring progress provides the objective data, and continuous improvement provides the proactive action. By embracing both as non-negotiable pillars of your journey, you ensure that your idea not only achieves its initial vision but continues to grow, adapt, and make a lasting, evolving impact in an ever-changing world. This ongoing journey of growth is the ultimate reward, transforming not just your ideas, but you, the creator, into a perpetually evolving force for positive change, leaving a legacy far beyond the initial concept. In the final conclusion, we will reflect on this powerful, holistic journey and the profound legacy you are building.

Conclusion

Your Ever-Evolving Masterpiece

You've reached the end of this book, but truly, you've just begun. Throughout these pages, we've embarked on a comprehensive journey, one that began not with an external task, but with a profound internal transformation. We started by cultivating the fertile ground of your mind, diligently unearthing limiting beliefs that once held you captive, embracing an unwavering optimism and robust resilience in the face of adversity, fueling an insatiable curiosity that drives continuous discovery, and learning the profound, often overlooked, power of self-compassion to sustain you through challenges. This foundational work was not merely beneficial; it was absolutely crucial, for it is from this rich, well-tended inner landscape that truly impactful, sustainable ideas can take root, flourish, and eventually bear fruit.

From that strong internal foundation, we then shifted our focus to the ideas themselves, the very seeds of your future impact. You learned to become a prolific idea generator, understanding with newfound clarity where those fleeting sparks of genius truly originate and how to systematically capture them. We then moved into the critical phase of shaping those raw concepts into clear, purposeful, and compelling visions, meticulously defining your unique "why" – the core purpose that transcends mere profit or recognition – and setting ambitious yet achievable goals that serve as your guiding stars. You courageously embraced the iterative journey of prototyping and testing, understanding deeply that imperfection is not a flaw to be hidden, but a necessary, invaluable step towards refinement and true market fit. We then equipped you with practical strategies to anticipate and proactively overcome obstacles, transforming what once seemed like insurmountable roadblocks into powerful stepping stones through creative problem-solving and adaptable thinking.

Finally, we moved decisively into the realm of action and tangible impact. You discovered how to break down daunting, seemingly overwhelming goals into smaller, more manageable, and immediately actionable steps, thereby dismantling procrastination and building unstoppable momentum. We explored the indispensable value of building a robust support system – actively seeking out wise mentors who can guide your path, collaborating with complementary talents who fill your skill gaps, and surrounding yourself with growth-minded individuals who uplift, inspire, and constructively challenge you. And in the preceding chapter, we delved into the vital, ongoing practices of defining success on your own terms, rigorously measuring progress with meaningful metrics, and committing wholeheartedly to continuous improvement, thereby ensuring your dedicated efforts lead to lasting, meaningful impact and sustained relevance.

The Journey Never Ends

If there's one overarching truth to carry forward from this book, one profound insight that underpins all the strategies and mindsets we've discussed, it is this: **the journey of growth—both for your ideas and for yourself—never truly ends.** There isn't a magical finish line, a final destination where you suddenly become "done" with growing, where all problems cease, and all learning concludes. Life is an inherently dynamic process, markets constantly evolve, technologies shift at an accelerating pace, and human needs and desires continuously change. To remain relevant, impactful, and deeply fulfilled, you must wholeheartedly embrace this continuous, lifelong state of evolution and adaptation.

This commitment to perpetual growth means:

- **Perpetual Learning:** The deep curiosity you've cultivated throughout this book is not a temporary tool; it is your lifelong companion and your most powerful asset. Keep reading voraciously across diverse fields, keep asking probing questions that challenge assumptions, keep exploring new disciplines and perspectives, and keep challenging your own ingrained beliefs and mental models. The moment you stop actively learning, the moment you assume you "know enough," is precisely the moment

you stop growing, and your ideas begin to stagnate. This means actively seeking out new information, engaging with diverse viewpoints, and maintaining a humble "beginner's mind" even as you gain expertise. It's about feeding your intellect consistently, like tending a vibrant garden.

- **Ongoing Adaptation:** Your ideas, like living organisms, are not static constructs. They are dynamic entities that must breathe, evolve, and respond to their environment. Be prepared to pivot your approach, refine your features, or even fundamentally reinvent your core offering as new information comes to light, as user feedback reveals deeper truths, or as the world around you undergoes significant shifts. Rigidity is the enemy of progress. Flexibility and agility are your superpowers, allowing you to navigate unforeseen challenges and seize emerging opportunities. This might mean letting go of a beloved feature that isn't resonating, or shifting your entire business model in response to a market disruption.

- **Relentless Self-Reflection:** Cultivate a consistent practice of checking in with your "why" and your core values. Are you still aligned with the deep purpose that initially fueled your idea? Are you still finding meaning and genuine fulfillment in the work you're doing? Are you nurturing your own well-being – your mental, emotional, and physical

health – as diligently as you nurture your ideas? This continuous internal audit ensures that your external pursuits remain in harmony with your internal state, preventing burnout and ensuring that your growth is holistic and sustainable. This might involve regular journaling, meditation, or simply dedicated quiet time for introspection.

- **Embracing the Next Challenge:** Once one significant goal is achieved, one mountain successfully climbed, resist the temptation to settle into a comfortable plateau. Instead, actively look for the next mountain to ascend, the next complex problem to solve, or the next exciting opportunity to explore. Growth comes from consistently pushing beyond your current limits, embracing discomfort, and seeking out new frontiers for learning and impact. This isn't about an endless, frantic pursuit, but a joyful, intentional engagement with the limitless possibilities of continuous development.

Embracing the Process of Growth

The true, enduring beauty and profound reward of this entire journey lies not just in the tangible outcomes you achieve – the successful product, the thriving business, the completed creative work – but even more so in the person you become along the way. The process of growing your ideas will inevitably stretch you in ways you never anticipated, challenge your assumptions about yourself

and the world, and reveal hidden strengths and capacities you never knew you possessed. It will also, with equal certainty, expose your vulnerabilities and areas for development, forcing you to cultivate even greater self-compassion, resilience, and adaptability. This transformation of self is the ultimate masterpiece.

Embracing the process means:

- **Valuing Effort Over Innate Talent (The Mastery Mindset):** Internalize the understanding that consistent, deliberate effort and persistent practice are far more powerful and predictive of long-term success than any perceived innate talent or "natural ability." Recognize that true mastery is built brick by brick, through countless hours of focused work, learning from mistakes, and continuous refinement. Your capacity for effort is your greatest asset.

- **Finding Joy in the Struggle and the Learning:** Shift your perspective to recognize that the most profound learning, the deepest insights, and the most significant personal growth often occur precisely during moments of difficulty, challenge, and even apparent failure. These are the crucibles where resilience is forged and creativity is sparked. Embrace the discomfort of learning and the grit required to push through, understanding that these moments are where true transformation happens.

- **Celebrating Every Step, Not Just the Summit:** Acknowledge and genuinely celebrate not just the big, public wins, but every small step forward, every tiny lesson learned, every minor obstacle overcome, and every consistent habit maintained. These "micro-celebrations" are vital for building momentum, reinforcing positive neural pathways, and sustaining motivation during the long haul. They remind you that progress, however incremental, is still progress.

- **Being Patient and Kind with Yourself:** Growth takes time. It is rarely linear. There will be inevitable setbacks, frustrating plateaus where progress seems to halt, and moments of profound doubt. Treat yourself with the same kindness, understanding, and persistence you would offer a cherished friend. Avoid harsh self-criticism. Understand that resilience means getting back up, not never falling. This self-compassion is the fuel for long-term endurance.

Your Legacy of Ideas and Mindset

As you continue to grow your ideas and cultivate your mindset, you are not merely building projects, launching businesses, or achieving personal goals; you are actively and consciously shaping your legacy. This legacy isn't necessarily about grand monuments, widespread fame, or immense wealth, though these may be outcomes. More

profoundly, it's about the lasting impact you create and the person you become in the process. It's a legacy built on contribution, courage, and continuous evolution.

It's about:

- **The Problems You Solved:** The tangible, real-world impact your ideas have on others' lives, alleviating pain points, creating joy, fostering connection, or driving progress. This is the measurable difference you make.

- **The Change You Created:** The positive ripples you send out into your community, your industry, or the wider world. This could be a new standard of ethical practice, a more inclusive product, a more sustainable process, or simply a spark of hope in someone's life.

- **The Person You Became:** The living embodiment of a growth mindset – resilient, curious, adaptable, compassionate, and action-oriented. Your transformed self is a testament to what's truly possible when one commits to continuous evolution and embraces the journey of becoming.

- **The Inspiration You Provide:** How your journey, your struggles, your triumphs, and your unwavering commitment to growth encourages and empowers others to grow their own ideas, overcome their own limiting beliefs, and unlock their unique potential. Your story becomes a beacon for those who follow.

This book has provided you with a comprehensive framework, a powerful set of tools, and a transformative shift in perspective. But the real work, the real magic, the real legacy, happens now, in your consistent, courageous, and compassionate action. Go forth, grow your ideas with purpose and passion, and let your ever-evolving mindset be the most magnificent masterpiece you ever create. The world is waiting, eagerly, for what you will bring to life next.

Keep Growing!